LOCOMOTION PAPERS

The EASINGWOLD RAILWAY

by

K.E. Hartley

Revised by

R.N. Redman

THE OAKWOOD PRESS

ISBN 0 85361 413 X

Typeset by Gem Publishing Company, Brightwell, Wallingford, Oxfordshire.

Printed by Alphaprint, Witney, Oxfordshire.

First Edition Published 1970

Second Enlarged Edition 1991

The tranquil scene of the market place, Easingwold c.1925. *Oakwood Collection*

Published by
The OAKWOOD PRESS
P.O.Box 122, Headington, Oxford.

Contents

Acknowledgements

1st Edition: By K.E. Hartley

My various visits to Easingwold have enabled me to obtain a fair amount of first-hand information, as well as data required for the preparation of the various drawings in this booklet. Nevertheless, much more knowledge has come to me from a wide variety of other sources, as indeed have many of the photographs in my collection.

My sincere thanks are especially due to Mrs M. Coates (the last Chairman of Directors) and her late husband, Mr G.H. Coates, for help, and access to certain company papers, also photographs; the BR Archivist, York; to members of York Reference Library staff; to the late Mr and Mrs Edward ('Jack') Morse, and the late Mr George Paragreen; and to Messrs G.E. Cowling, C.R. Evers, K. Hoole, G. Horsman, E.A. Hudson, R.J. Hunter, J.B. Stork, H. Osborne, R.N. Redman, T.E. Rounthwaite, M. Wilson and G. Woodcock, for information and for photographs.

Grateful acknowledgement is made to *The Railway Magazine*, *Locomotive Magazine*, *BR Magazine*, and *The Dalesman*, for the use of certain material from their pages; and, similarly, to *The Easingwold Advertiser*, *The Northern Echo*, *Sunday Dispatch*, *Yorkshire Gazette*, *Yorks Evening Press*, and *The Yorkshire Post*.

2nd Edition: By R.N. Redman

On numerous visits to the line and its area I met many people with fond memories of the little railway and their stories and recollections have added a lot of snippets of information and local colour.

My sincere thanks are particularly due to Mr Samuel Morse, an authority on the Easingwold area and its railway. He is the only surviving son of Edward (Jack) Morse, and he made his knowledge freely available to me during our long chats, adding much interesting detail to sections of this book.

In conclusion I would like to acknowledge the assistance of Messrs E.G. Cope, C.R. Evers, G. Horsman, A. Lawson, H.M. Pattison and P.S. Halton, the latter being responsible for the drawing of Locomotive No. 2.

A well loaded North Eastern Railway 'Londonderry' steam wagon in Easingwold station yard *c.*1912. *R.J. Hunter Collection*

3452 EASINGWOLD RAILWAY 3452
FOR CONDITIONS SEE BACK. Available for three days including day of issue
EASINGWOLD TO
ALNE
Fare SECOND / S. 3154 ALNE \ 7½d.C CLASS

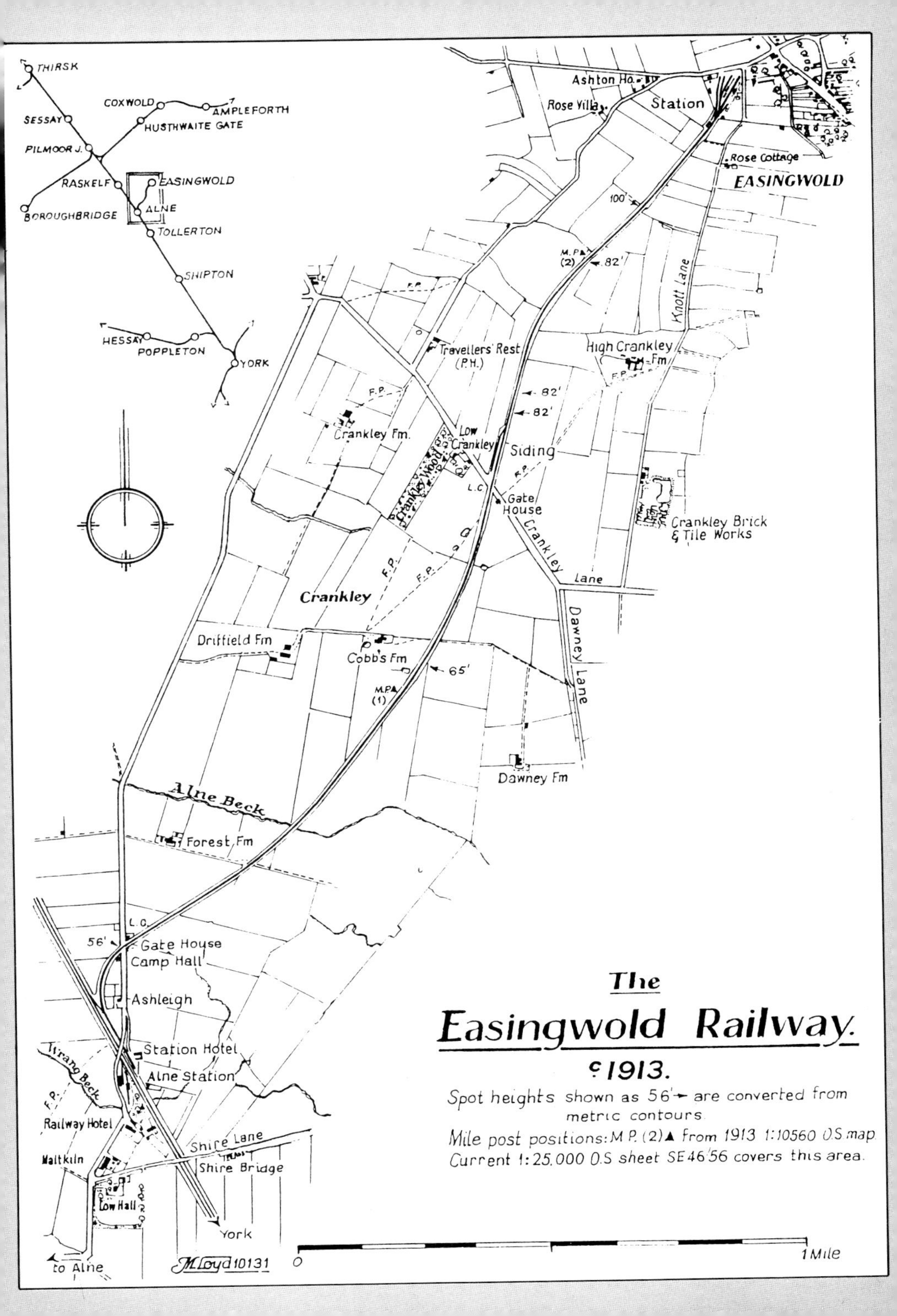
THIRSK
COXWOLD
AMPLEFORTH
SESSAY
HUSTHWAITE GATE
PILMOOR J.
RASKELF
EASINGWOLD
ALNE
BOROUGHBRIDGE
TOLLERTON
SHIPTON
HESSAY
POPPLETON
YORK
Ashton Ho.
Rose Villa
Station
Rose Cottage
EASINGWOLD
100'
M.P. (2)
82'
Knott Lane
F.P.
Travellers' Rest (P.H.)
High Crankley Fm
82'
82'
Crankley Fm.
Low Crankley
Siding
Crankley Wood
L.C.
Gate House
Crankley Lane
Crankley Brick & Tile Works
Crankley
Dawney Lane
Driffield Fm
Cobb's Fm
65'
M.P. (1)
Dawney Fm
Alne Beck
Forest Fm
L.C.
56'
Gate House
Camp Hall
Ashleigh
Station Hotel
Alne Station
Wrang Beck
Railway Hotel
Shire Lane
Maltkiln
Shire Bridge
Low Hall
York
to Alne
M.Loyd 10131
0
1 Mile
The Easingwold Railway.
c1913.
Spot heights shown as 56' are converted from metric contours.
Mile post positions: M.P. (2) from 1913 1:10560 O.S. map.
Current 1:25,000 O.S sheet SE 46/56 covers this area.

Hudswell Clarke 0–6–0ST locomotive *Easingwold* and two vintage ex-North Eastern Railway coaches pose just out from Alne Station in this fine turn-of-the-century view.
K.E. Hartley Collection

Foreword

To be asked to edit a new enlarged edition of Ken Hartley's 1970 history of the Easingwold Railway is a pleasure tinged with a little sadness. Ken was the doyen of Yorkshire's minor railway historians and apart from numerous articles, completed four detailed histories before his death in 1984 at the age of 77.

At the time of the first edition it was the first detailed coverage of this delightful 2½ mile long railway byway, a true pioneer of the standard gauge light railway and often referred to as 'England's shortest standard gauge passenger line'.

In its planning and construction, the far-sighted sponsors shrewdly anticipated by some years, the Light Railways Act of 1896. Indeed, during the passage through Parliament of this Bill, the Easingwold Railway was prominently before the Committee, and its operation closely studied. Moreover, unlike a number of light railways later constructed under the Act, the Easingwold Railway was, on the whole, a reasonably successful financial undertaking. Although it finally had to close – after outliving almost all other small independent standard gauge lines in the country – this was largely brought about by changing trends in transport and the vast development of road haulage, changes which have also seriously affected railways in many other parts of the world.

'The Easingwold' was not a spectacular railway, but when it closed it left behind a proud record of 66 years of honest service to the community, and an abiding affection among those who knew it. There are still many people who recall the little railway, and regret its disappearance – nor are they all 'railway enthusiasts'.

Ken's long association with the line went back to 1913, when at the age of 12 his father introduced him to engine No. 2. This first contact must have made quite an impression for in 1921 he walked from York to Alne to join the train. This was probably the most memorable of countless visits for, to quote his own words, 'after haunting the station and staff at Easingwold most of the afternoon, I returned on the 3 pm train to Alne, when the driver Jack Morse invited me into the cab of No. 2, while he went over to the goods yard to pick up some wagons for the return trip to Easingwold. This my very first ride on a locomotive, was a thrill indeed'.

He went on to recall his first meeting with the late Mr G.H. Coates the line's long serving Secretary and Manager, in 1930, 'When I told him that I had set off in pouring rain at 5 am from Elland for a round trip by cycle of 110 miles, expressly to visit and photograph the railway, he became very interested and co-operative and suggested riding the train one way and walking back along the track so that I should see everything of interest'.

Right up to the very end of the railway, Ken made regular visits by cycle, scooter and train to sketch, photograph and just soak up the atmosphere – the following text is testimony to his research and enthusiasm.

Ronald Nelson Redman
Horsforth, Leeds
November 1990

A fine posed scene at Easingwold station (*c.*1904) with locomotive No. 2 and the new ex-North London coaches. Second from left is porter Wilf Pettinger, then to the right Jack Morse; George Paragreen. Sitting on locomotive: Dolly Frankland, ?, Hugh Morse, ?. The driver was Jack Danby and the gentleman in the boater is Dr E.B. Hicks.

Mrs M. Coates Collection

Chapter One

Introduction and Historical

Thirteen miles north of York on the A19 main road to Middlesbrough lies the very attractive little market town of Easingwold, set in the fertile Vale of York. Ten miles to the north-west, is Thirsk in the shadow of the Hambleton Hills and the famous Yorkshire 'White Horse'. Nearer and to the north are Byland Abbey and nearby Coxwold, famed as the home of Laurence Sterne, and the ruined castle of Sheriff Hutton is just over to the east.

A very pleasant place is Easingwold, with a faintly old world air of quiet prosperity. There is a market place of two acres and numerous attractive Georgian residences within easy reach of the wide main thoroughfare, aptly named Long Street, which rises slightly to the crossroads at its northern extremity. Turn right here up a gentle slope, and you will come to the solidly-built church and the manor house. A short distance down the left turn, Raskelf Road, will lead you to what was once the terminus of the Easingwold Railway. Only the street name, Station Court, will give a clue to the site, now almost entirely covered with new housing.

Still standing is the imposing Station Hotel, dating back to 1892. This building formed the backdrop to so many early photographs of the railway, where countless pints must have been sold to thirsty railway men and enthusiasts over the years.

It is agriculture that has always been the mainspring of the town's activities and prosperity, although for many years it was noted for the manufacture of 'steels' used for cutlery purposes. These were made by the firm of Barker, a family business, in the market place. Founded in the early part of the 19th century, the firm received honourable mention for their exhibit of Butchers' and Household steels at the Great Exhibition of 1851, in the Crystal Palace, and later had international connections.

The progressive people of Easingwold early recognised the advantages of being in rail communication with the rest of the country, for it appears that agitation for a railway started as early as 1836, with the passing of the Great North of England Rly Act, and an Easingwold attorney, one Robert Gill (1807–1893), who for a time practised in the Tolbooth, in the market place, tried to get the York–Darlington line brought, if not through, then at least nearer to, the town. He was unsuccessful in this attempt; but the idea of a railway lingered on, and a Guide Book of 1843, with the ponderous title of *A Brief Description of Places of Public Interest in the County of York within 26 miles of the City* tells us that 'The Alne station of the GN of E Rly is distant from Easingwold about 3 miles, and it is in contemplation to form a line from that station to the town, which no doubt will add much to the improvement of the place'.

Two years later, a certain John Plummer, of New Parks, and owner of a well-known racing mare, 'Alice Hawthorn', is said to have offered the inhabitants of Easingwold the whole of the mare's winnings, for one year, on the condition that they built a railway from Easingwold to connect with the GN of E Rly. Not surprisingly, this quaint proposal failed to produce the desired result. Bradshaw's 'Map of Great Britain, showing the Railways completed and in progress' (1851) indicated a line direct from the vicinity of

Pilmoor Junction to Easingwold, but in fact, this railway was never built. A writer in the *Easingwold Times*, on the opening of the Town Hall, in 1864, commented 'Now all we need is a branch railway'. The desire for a line remained!

In the early 1860s the London & North Western Railway, with its eye on the lucrative coal traffic of N.E. England, proposed to build a line from the West Riding to Teeside, passing through Easingwold *en route*. This did not, of course, materialise, and it was not until 1880, when a long letter from a Mr F.E. Rookledge, of Easingwold, appeared in the *Yorkshire Post and Leeds Intelligencer*', advocating a branch line from Alne, that a faint hint of ultimate success began to appear. During the next few years, some real progress was evident, when a number of leading landowners and residents in the area got together, and applied to Parliament for an Act to construct a railway from Alne station to Easingwold. This was passed in 1887, and the Company was incorporated on 23rd August, 1887.

The following portion of the Easingwold Railway Act describes the railway as shown on the original plans presented to Parliament:

> A Railway (No. 1) – [Nos 2 and 3 are the sidings and spur connecting with the North Eastern main line at Alne] two miles three furlongs and four chains in length commencing in the parish of Alne at the northern fence of a field belonging or reputed to belong to William Severs and occupied by Jane Hutton Prest at a point eighty yards or thereabouts measured along the said fence from the highway leading from Alne to Easingwold and terminating on the south-west side of Long Street in the town and parish of Easingwold at a point in a garden belonging or reputed to belong to and occupied by John Buckle distant twenty yards or thereabouts in a westerly direction from the door opening from the said garden into Long Street aforesaid.

It would appear that during the time between the application for, and the granting of, the Act, there had been some further thought on the route to be taken by the railway, and the position of its terminus, for a Detailed Report prepared by a Mr Copperthwaite, Junr, indicated a new, and cheaper, location for the station at Easingwold, which was originally intended to be centrally and conveniently situated at the back of Long Street.

THE PROPOSED EASINGWOLD RAILWAY.

PUBLIC MEETING AT EASINGWOLD.

Extracted from the "York Daily Herald" of Saturday, October 8th, 1887.

Yesterday evening, a public meeting was held in the Town Hall, Easingwold, for the purpose of taking the necessary steps for putting into force the powers of the Easingwold Railway Act, 1887. There was a large attendance of the inhabitants of Easingwold and the district.

Sir GEORGE O. WOMBWELL, Bart., presided, and after reading the circular convening the meeting, said many efforts had been made to obtain a railway to Easingwold, but he was sorry to say, that hitherto they had all failed. Now Parliament had granted the necessary powers, and he thought the time had arrived for everybody who took an interest in the welfare of Easingwold to do the best they could to enable the line to be made, by subscribing the necessary capital. It was greatly to be hoped that the landowners in the neighbourhood would come forward and subscribe what they could in order to facilitate the carrying out of that important undertaking, which he need hardly say would be a great advantage to the town of Easingwold. It was proposed to construct the line as cheaply as possible, consistent with safety and utility. The North-Eastern

Railway Company had met the promoters in the most friendly spirit — (applause), — and had promised to assist in any way they possibly could. So he really thought there was at last a chance that the railroad which had been so long talked about would be made. He should be very glad to take shares, and he knew several of his friends who would also take some. (Applause.) He hoped they would see their way to support the scheme. He then called upon Mr Robinson to give some statistical information.

Mr. O. ROBINSON, of Easingwold, said they were fortunate in having obtained Parliamentary powers for the construction of a railway from Alne, and they were further fortunate in having obtained from Mr. Copperthwaite, junior, a report, which is as follows:—

In accordance with the arrangements made with you at our interview in May last, I have the honour to lay before you the detailed estimate for the engineering work necessary for the construction of a railway from Alne Station to Easingwold, and a further summary of the other expenses necessary to the complete equipment of the line for public traffic. The total amount of capital expenditure, exclusive of professional charges, I estimate at £8,783, which sum is made up as follows:— Contract for engineering work, £5,136 13*s.* 11*d.*; North-Eastern Railway charge in connection with Alne Railway, £312; locomotive, &c., account, £1,035; four cottages, £600; land, twelve acres, £1,200; tools, furniture, &c., £500; total, £8,783 13*s.* 11*d.* The contract sum includes all work shown on the plans. The cost of the four cottages is not included in this sum as they are not absolutely necessary, and in any case would probably be built more cheaply by a local builder. The sum to be paid to the North-Eastern Railway Company comprises the cost of signal alterations which would be required to protect the junction with the Easingwold line, and the price of second - hand permanent way material for the New Station-yard at Alne, which would be supplied to the contractor. The sum of £1,035 for locomotive, &c., stock includes the price of a light tank engine, two second-hand carriages, a weigh machine for Easingwold Station, and a water crane for Alne. The amount of land required is about 12 acres. The sum of £500 for tools, &c., is intended to include all the charges incidental to starting the railway as a working concern. The amount of the contract sum which heads the above list is determined by the following considerations:– 1. Economy as far as is consistent with a reasonable regard for the restriction of revenue charges for repairs and maintenance within due limits. 2. The permanent way is designed to carry light engines only and drawing short trains. 3. The offices, &c., are to be wooden buildings on brick foundations. 4. The station-yard at Easingwold is laid out with coal depôts, offices, goods wharf, and passenger platforms, and is arranged so as to admit of extension should the traffic require it. 5. The station yard at Alne is arranged so that waggons coming over the North-Eastern line can be shunted into the Easingwold Company's yard and then taken up by the light engine. The passenger train from Easingwold will run to the existing platform at Alne. These arrangements will involve a sharing of the expenses incurred by the North-Eastern Railway Company at Alne Station in proportion to the traffic done. An agreement of this kind with the North-Eastern Railway Company will, I am convinced, be found much less costly than the maintenance by the Easingwold Railway Company of a separate staff at Alne. With regard to the request contained in the letter of September 12 from Messrs. Robinson and Son, that I should estimate the extra cost involved in placing the Easingwold terminus in its original position as shown on the Parliamentary plan, I have to report that an increase of at least £1,300 would have to be made to the above total of £8,783. Such an alteration would, of course, involve a complete re-arrangement of the gradients of the line as at present laid out.

The railway, Mr. Robinson said, will accommodate the inhabitants of the following places: Easingwold 2,044, Stillington 600, Craike 501, Brandsby and Stearsby 300, Oulston 177, Yearsley 161, Thormanby 135, Thornton Hill 50, Boascar 30, giving a total population of 4,000. There is a weekly corn market attended by corn-factors from Leeds and York. There are also artificial manure merchants, hay buyers, wool buyers, potato merchants, fruit dealers, and other persons engaged in agriculture who resort to Easingwold at various times during the year from all parts of the country. The hirings at Martinmas and the annual Agricultural Show in September also attracted a good many visitors. Easingwold is a centre for all local business within a wide area, including County Court, Highway Board, Magisterial, and Poor Law business, and is necessarily resorted to for these purposes by many parties during the year who had to come in the first instance to Alne station. There are various carts from the principal places in the district to York who carry a large number of passengers during the year, and the bulk of these passengers may fairly be claimed for the new railway. Better access to Easingwold as the centre of the district would inevitably lead to the town and its neighbourhood being more resorted to by outsiders, and in all probability persons having business in York and other towns would begin to reside at Easingwold, and the vicinity, as is already the case at Alne, &c. Altogether, therefore, it may reasonably be assumed that there would be a good and steady passenger traffic for the new railway to begin with, and one that would increase materially in the future. There would be no reason why the trains on the new line should not run in connection with all stopping trains on the main line. The principal revenue of the line would no doubt be derived from the carriage of agricultural produce, coal, lime, timber, and general goods traffic. The total area of the district which the railway will accommodate is about 21,000 acres, and the chief articles of cultivation are wheat, barley, oats, rye, beans, peas, potatoes, turnips, mangolds, carrots, and hay. At a low estimate it may be assumed that at least 8,000 tons of agricultural produce will be annually sent by rail out of the district. This does not include wool and cattle, nor agricultural machinery. A considerable quantity of lime, artificial manures, soot, road metal and building materials come into the district from the existing stations at Alne, Tollerton, and Raskelf, and the bulk would no doubt come over the new line to Easingwold. The general goods traffic into the town is at least 1,000 tons in weight, and the coal consumed in the district, and which would no doubt all come in the first instance to Easingwold station, averages 10,000 tons per annum. It may fairly be considered, therefore, that there is an existing traffic for the line of all kinds of traffic (other than passenger traffic) of at least 25,000 tons per annum. This traffic, allowing a moderate terminal at Easingwold, should produce at least £1,400 per annum, and taking the passenger traffic at £600 per annum there should be a gross revenue of £2,000 a year for the new railway, allowing 55 per cent. for working expenses, and this would leave £900 for debenture interest and dividend; and after paying 4 per cent. on the £4,000 worth of debentures, and 5 per cent. on the paid-up share capital, would leave a balance to be placed to reserve. Working plans and drawings for the line have been prepared by Mr. Copperthwaite, jun., and he has also prepared an estimate for the construction and equipment of the line at a total cost, including the purchase of the land, of £8,783 13*s.* 11*d.* A contractor of good standing is prepared to undertake the works on the basis of Mr. Copperthwaite's estimate, and to subscribe £1,000 toward the share capital. The cost of obtaining the Act had been kept within the narrowest limits, and amounts to £550, and the Parliamentary deposit of 5 per cent. on the estimate has been invested in £681 16*s.* 6*d.* new 2½ per cent. annuities, and is now deposited with the Paymaster-General and forms part of the capital of the company, and will be refunded to them when the line is constructed. The total length of the line is 2 miles and 28 chains, and it is confidently expected that £10,000 will cover the entire cost of construction and equipment. They were informed by Mr. Copperthwaite that he had made his report on how the line could be constructed in the cheapest possible manner, and at the same time to secure thorough efficiency of working powers. They had heard the general facts, and it was for them to say whether they would give their support to the scheme put before them. A house to house inquiry had been made as to the amount of coals used; and as to land produce, the return of the Board of Trade had been obtained from the excise officers at York.

Mr. BAKER, LONDON, the solicitor to the Company, then made a statement as to the cost of construction of similar railway lines and the results of their working, and said it was proposed to raise £12,000 capital by the issue of 1,200 shares of £10 each, and they had powers to borrow £4,000. Mr. Copperthwaite had estimated that the line would cost under £9,000, and he should like to see it constructed without any resort to borrowing powers, which would then remain in their possession if they wished to exercise them at any time they liked to do so. The contractor stated that he could make the line by Christmas. The line could be made quickly and cheaply, because it was only a surface line. The Parliamentary plan put the station in Long-street, but according to Mr. Copperthwaite's plan it would be in the Vicarage field. It was for the inhabitants to say where the station would be most convenient. Of course, they had to consider economy in the matter. To place the station in Long Street would cost £1,300 more.

The Rev. Father PEARSON, speaking upon the question as to the site of the Easingwold Station, said he thought that the extra money would be well spent if they had to have it in Long Street, so that visitors to Easingwold would be brought into the town.

Mr. BAKER, in reply, expressed himself in favour of that view, but reminded them that it would be at an extra cost of £1,300.

In the course of some conversation which ensued, it was stated that a prospectus would be issued.

On the proposition of the Rev. Father PEARSON, seconded by the Rev. N. JACKSON, a vote of thanks was passed to Sir George Wombwell for presiding and the meeting terminated.

A detailed report of the meeting re the Easingwold Railway.

From the Prospectus mentioned in the above newspaper report, we learn that the original Directors, four in number, were: Sir George Orby Wombwell, Bart, Newburgh Priory, Easingwold; Joseph Horatio Love, Esq., J.P. Hawkhills, Easingwold; George Hudson Smith, Easingwold; The Hon. Francis Herbert Dawnay, Beningbrough Hall, York; R.E. Cooper, Esq., M.I.C.E., Parliament St., Westminster, S.W., was the Consulting Engineer. The Prospectus also informed its readers that, 'The estimated time of construction of the line was no more than 3 months, while due to the low cost of labour and material, competitive contracts were to be obtained on very favourable terms'.

It is not known how long elapsed before the necessary capital became available, although the early application for shares appears to have been good. In due course, tenders were invited for the building of the railway. Details are not available of all these, but it is known that Henry C. Pauling, 66, Basinghall St, London E.C., submitted the following figures: 'As per Copperthwaite proposals, £6,176. As per Parliamentary Drawings, to Long Street, including a road bridge and approach, £7,275'. It has been stated that the Contract was originally awarded to a firm by the ominous-sounding name of Death & Co., which failed when only half the work was completed, and consequently another (unknown) contractor was appointed to finish the job. This was finally accomplished by the middle of 1891 – nearly four years after that momentous meeting in Easingwold Town Hall.

But the good people of Easingwold, whatever they might have thought about this long delay, were determined that their Railway should be opened with due celebrations, and the event took place on Saturday 25th July, 1891. The driver of the first train from Alne to Easingwold was Mr Sidney Smith, son of Director G.H. Smith. Then still a young man in his teens, he took over the controls of the little Hudswell Clarke saddle-tank from the NER men, at Alne.

The *York Evening Press*, for Monday 27th July, 1891 carried this report of the proceedings:

OPENING OF THE EASINGWOLD RAILWAY

Saturday was a red letter day at Easingwold, the great event being the opening of the new railway. Although the line will not properly be used by the travelling public until this morning, yet passenger trains were running pretty nearly all day on Saturday.

The Directors decided to celebrate the opening by giving the school children and teachers of the town a free ride to Alne Junction and back, and this was no small matter with the juveniles, considering that many of them probably had never seen a train in their lives. Nor were the older people indifferent to the proceedings of this joyful day, for they assembled at the Easingwold terminus in large numbers to witness the arrival and departure of the trains.

The children, about 400, assembled at the various schools in the town and proceeded to the station decorated with flags and banners. The train which was provided consisted of an engine and two carriages, and about 100 children, teachers, etc., were carried each time the train made an excursion, the return journey occupying about 25 minutes. Mr G.H. Smith, one of the Managing Directors, the Vicar of Easingwold (the Rev. N. Jackson), Inspector Alexander, and other gentlemen, were present to assist the Station Master (Mr Thornton). There was immense cheering as the whistle of the engine announced the movement of the train.

At 4 o'clock, tea was provided for the children and teachers in the Market Hall by the Easingwold Sports Committee, and at the conclusion . . . three cheers were given for the Directors for the trips over the line, and to the ladies and gentlemen . . . for the excellent tea.

Afterwards, through the great kindness of the Vicar, the children, teachers and friends were admitted to the beautiful grounds of the Vicarage on Church Hill, which was highly appreciated by both young and old.

The proceedings ended at about 8 pm, with the singing of the National Anthem – but the day will long be remembered as one of the most important in the history of the old North Riding town of Easingwold. On Monday 27th

North Eastern Railway, Londonderry steam wagon No. 6 (BT 204), a product of the Seaham Harbour Works, photographed in 1905 outside the railway fire engine house in York. This design was later fitted with a roof canopy and at least one worked out of Easingwold station yard. *Ken Hoole Collection*

Another North Eastern steam wagon, BT 203, outside fire engine house No. 1, this time a 'St Pancras' model. *Ken Hoole Collection*

July, 1891, the Easingwold Railway officially settled down to business, and no longer were the townspeople dependent on the slow carrier's cart or the little two-horse omnibus which three times daily made the return trip between 'The George Hotel & Posting House' in the Market Place, Easingwold, and Alne, driven by Henry Harper or his assistant Arthur Swan.

Mr James Haynes the proprietor of 'The George' and its omnibus service offered his customers East India Pale and Light dinner ales, Guinness Dublin stout and ales and porter in six gallon casks and upwards. He soon changed his bus service to 'Omnibus to and from Easingwold Station'. The service could be handy if the railway ran into problems, and an invoice dated 2nd September, 1891 to the Easingwold Railway Co. was for taking 10 passengers to Alne Station (6*s*.), in addition to a previous outstanding account for (4s.), total 10*s*. This was finally settled by the Railway Company on 29th December – cash flow problems are not a new phenomena after all!

The *Yorkshire Gazette* for Saturday 1st August, 1891, also featured a generally similar report of the opening of the railway, and stated that both goods and passenger traffic were progressing very satisfactorily, and also that 'on Thursday next the opening of the railway will be further celebrated by Athletic Sports, a Firework Display, etc.' Thus at long last, Easingwold got its own little railway, which was to serve the town and its area for the next 66 years in good times and bad. The only mystery arising from all this euphoria and celebration is the apparent total absence of any photographs of the opening day events or the first train, and in particular the short-lived, tiny four-coupled locomotive which struggled to provide a regular service.

Dr E.B. Hicks Secretary and General Manager of the Easingwold Railway from 1893 to 1925. He doubled up as Medical Officer for Easingwold and remained in general practice. *K.E. Hartley Collection*

Alne station looking north (down the main line) with the Easingwold bay on the right hand side. Note the semi-waterlogged lane down to the light railway and there is rather less shine on the Easingwold rails than the East Coast 'speed track'. The NE Railway has had obvious problems with the siting of the signal on the down line near the overbridge. *Locomotive Publishing Co.*

August 1937 and Easingwold No. 2 trundles down the side of the main line with the afternoon train from Alne. The coach is the ex-North Eastern brake composite coach No. 2442. *K.E. Hartley*

Chapter Two

The Railway Described

The Easingwold Railway started from a bay at the northern end of the up platform at Alne Station, on the main line from York to the North. Indeed, the Easingwold Railway platform – very narrow in width – extended a short distance beyond that of the NER, and actually had its ramp end under the bridge carrying the road from Alne to Easingwold over the various tracks.

At one time (it was certainly there in 1921) a simple water column stood on the other side of the track in the bay platform, and was similar to the one at Easingwold station. It seems to have been removed sometime in the 1930s, however. Immediately beyond the road bridge was a run-round loop, and a long siding. The loop sent off a trailing connection with the up main line and, at its farther end, the single line track of the Easingwold Railway bore away sharply to the right, and almost at once passed over the Easingwold road by means of a level crossing, the keeper of which lived in a neat cottage adjacent to the gates.

It should be mentioned that, in the mid-1930s, Alne Station was to some extent re-modelled, to accommodate a third 'through' line, and the crossover and access lines to the goods yard (which was situated on the down side) were re-positioned – a change which entailed some extra running for the Easingwold locomotive and its crew.

Beyond the level crossing, the railway ran straight for about ⅜ mile, and then, by means of a simple bridge of about 10 ft span, crossed a small stream, the water of which eventually reached the North Sea by way of the rivers Kyle, Ouse and Humber. Continuing for roughly another ⅞ mile, in a generally north-easterly direction, and veering very slightly to the left, the line crossed a second road on the level, at Crankley. The gates and cottage here were very similar to those at the Alne crossing, but beyond the road, with its 'dead end' adjacent to the gates, was a single siding – latterly little used – locked and controlled by an Annett's Key, carried on the train.

The line now curved gradually to the right for a short distance and then continued straight on until near to the little engine shed, where it bore slightly to the left as it entered the spacious yard at Easingwold, and finished up at the buffer stops at the platform end, 2 miles and 37 chains from Alne.

Beside the engine shed, a line led off to the right, up a bank, to serve the coal drops, and a few yards further on were the points for the long run-round loop, from which access was gained to the various lines of sidings, and to the engine shed. There were four sidings – not three, as stated in some magazine articles. This fact is borne out by personal observation, and lay-out plans made in both 1921 and 1931, and corroborated by the relative Ordnance Survey sheet, 1/2500 scale. The outermost siding served not only a loading platform, adjacent to Raskelf road, but also a large coaling stage built of sleepers, and gave off a spur which led to the engine shed. The next siding served the other face of this platform, which was rebuilt and faced in concrete, about 1944.

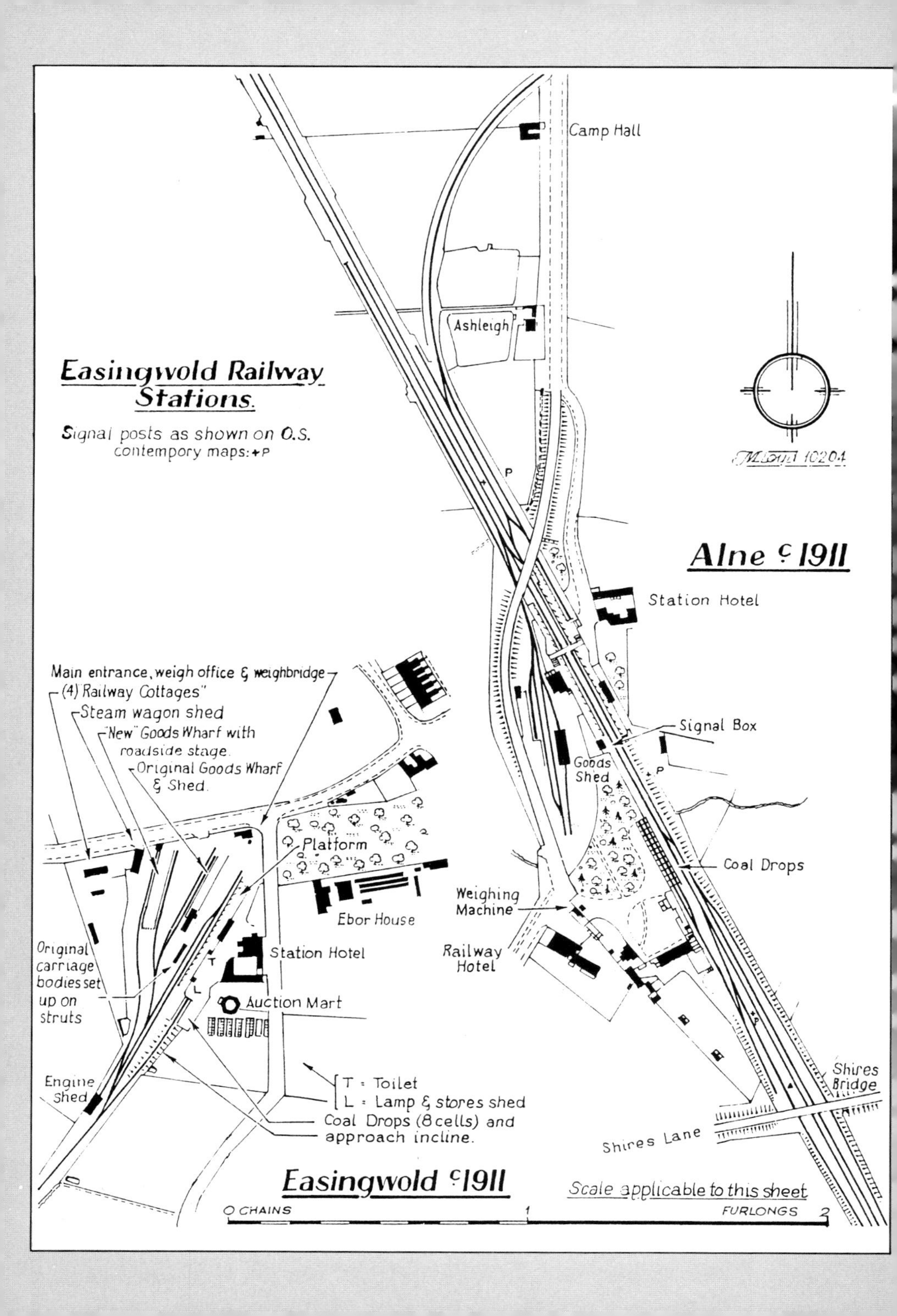

Easingwold Railway Stations.
Signal posts as shown on O.S. contempory maps: +P
Camp Hall
Ashleigh
P
Alne c 1911
Station Hotel
Signal Box
Goods Shed
P
Coal Drops
Weighing Machine
Railway Hotel
Shires Bridge
Shires Lane
Main entrance, weigh office & weighbridge
(4) Railway Cottages"
Steam wagon shed
"New" Goods Wharf with roadside stage.
Original Goods Wharf & Shed.
Platform
Ebor House
Station Hotel
Original carriage bodies set up on struts
T
L
Auction Mart
Engine Shed
T = Toilet
L = Lamp & stores shed
Coal Drops (8 cells) and approach incline.
Easingwold c 1911
Scale applicable to this sheet
0 CHAINS
1
FURLONGS
2

Locomotive No. 2, with proud driver and train, waiting for the rush of passengers in the bay platform at Alne Station! *R.C. Riley Collection*

High summer idyll – all the charm of pre-war light railways caught in this 1937 study of Easingwold No. 2, with the Saturday afternoon train at Alne Station. All that remains today is the Station Hotel building, externally little altered but no longer a hotel. *K.E. Hartley*

BR No. 68726 rests in the Alne bay platform after the Branch Line Society Special on 2nd June, 1957. Worthy of note are the superb platform lamp post with its oil lamp and the metal Virol sign, then quite commonplace – now both collector's items.
R.M. Casserley

A further view of the Branch Line Society Special hauled by No. 68726 having just arrived back at Alne, on Sunday 2nd June, 1957. 'The Yorkshire Man' headboard on the main line locomotive is just visible at the bottom right. This was class 'D20' 4–4–0 No. 62387.
H.C. Casserley

The other two sidings were close together, the inner one serving the goods shed platform and cattle dock. This, presumably, would be the 'goods wharf' mentioned in the Report of 1887. The goods shed itself, 38 ft long, by 14 ft 3 in. wide, was originally a round-topped structure of corrugated iron, with a large sliding door on each side, and a lean-to extension, 9 ft 6 in. by 14 ft 3 in., built across the end. It is possible that the building was not erected at the opening of the railway, for the *Locomotive Magazine* dated 15th March, 1912, does not mention it, but states 'For the goods traffic, a store has been made from two old NER carriages formerly used on the line'.

For a number of years, the shed was painted dark red, like the two old coaches, but both it and the latter had usually weathered to a deep pink shade, whenever I saw them! During the latter part of World War II, this shed was partly re-sheeted, and a normal 'Vee' roof fitted, in corrugated asbestos, and the walls were finished in black.

Facing this 'goods wharf', at the other side of the loop line, was the neat little passenger station, with a rather low, brick-faced platform, about 300 ft in length. The station building, which comprised the Secretary's office, station master's office, etc., also had a large lobby, in which passengers could wait, and obtain tickets, but I do not recollect ever seeing any seats. It was 50 ft long, by 13 ft wide, built of timber, and set on a brick base – precisely as per the Copperthwaite proposals. That it was soundly constructed, in the first place, was evident from its condition, even early in 1967 – ten years after the closure. The colour scheme was buff, with white window frames, and light brown doors, with buff panels – though latterly, the window surrounds were a red-brown shade, only the sash-bars being white. The roof was covered with slates. Unfortunately, on 13th June, 1967, this building was completely destroyed by a fire, the origin of which has not been discovered. A somewhat elementary 'toilet', and a small lamp room – both of timber, and painted buff – also had a place on the platform, which was backed by a neat white-painted fence. These two little buildings were completely rebuilt in 1944.

The roadway serving the rear of the station was also the approach to the coal drops, and to the Auction Mart, 0.91 acre in extent, which was another property owned by the company. At the main gateway to the station yard was the slate-roofed, timber-built 'weigh office'; the weighbridge itself was still there in 1969. The finish of this building was similar to that of the station offices.

At the second entrance to the goods yard, there was formerly another large shed, of corrugated iron. This had evidently been extended at some time, for whereas the older portion had a slate roof, the new part was covered with corrugated iron. This building was once used to house a North Eastern Railway steam wagon, which operated a road motor service to the Brandsby area in the earlier years, and had a pit to facilitate servicing operations. It was demolished some time after the closure, and the pit filled in.

One more building remains to be mentioned – the locomotive shed. This little brick building, approximately 36 ft long by 15 ft 6 in. wide, had a red pantile roof, with one or two tiles of thick glass and, particularly in the last

A view from under the bridge at Alne station showing locomotive No. 2 in the sylvan setting of the bay platform, a 2nd class compartment door open for any customers who may turn up. *Lens of Sutton*

BR class 'J72' No. 68726 with the Branch Line Society Special on Sunday 2nd June, 1957 standing by the overbridge at Alne. *R.M. Casserley*

Crossing gates and cottage where the line crossed the Easingwold road near Alne, Summer, 1930. *K.E. Hartley*

Crankley Crossing in 1947. The track is getting quite grassy but not as overgrown as the disused siding practically invisible on the right hand side. *R.N. Redman Collection*

A general view of Easingwold station yard on 13th August, 1949 from the coal drops. One wagon and two vans stand on the goods line. Note the rather over-ambitious length of the station platform. *K.E. Hartley*

A view that captures all the charm of an English light railway – locomotive No. 2 and coach at the platform. The station toilet is showing its age and developing a distinct list. The track in the loop is in good condition with newish looking sleepers but has the usual lack of ash ballast. Ex-North Eastern coach body, mounted on timber piles, can be seen at left. *Photomatic Ltd*

A view rarely photographed – the back of Easingwold station seen on 20th August, 1952. The road to the coal drops was to the right and to the left was the auction market. Note the new stove pipe chimney fitted to the station office, by this time used by a potato merchant. *K.E. Hartley*

An interesting very early view of Easingwold station from the buffers with the Station Hotel dated 1892, prominent to the left. An attractive building, it has been little altered to the present time. *Lens of Sutton*

The two original coaches standing in Easingwold station, with the Station Hotel at the rear. The station fencing boasts an attractive display of early metal signs.

Lens of Sutton

The shadows lengthen in this 1930s study of a slumbering station. The wooden structure in the foreground is the toilet. To economise, the high mounted oil lamp was intended to illuminate fitfully the toilet block interior as well as the platform area.

K.E. Hartley

years, with the grass-grown tracks and foliage of nearby trees, had a delightfully 'rural' aspect.

A single window in each side, and one in the end opposite the doors, served to light it and a long pit was provided for maintenance work. In one corner, there was a forge, and, across the end wall, a substantial bench, while on the side adjacent to the 'main line', there was a 3-ram force pump driven by a petrol/paraffin engine, which was used for boiler washing-out. The double doors were of timber, 10ft 4in. in overall width, and no more than 12 ft from rail level.

This was indeed a miniature engine shed, and while it was entirely adequate when the Easingwold Railway had its own motive power, it was unable to admit any locomotives subsequently hired from the LNER and BR, as these were at least a foot too high to pass under the door opening. Consequently, the 0–6–0Ts of classes 'J71' and 'J72' had to 'sleep rough', parked on the 'main line', alongside the shed, with a piece of old tarpaulin, or sacking, as the only 'protection' for the footplate against rain and snow.

The water supply at Easingwold took the form of a metal pipe of about 3 in. bore, shaped roughly like an inverted 'L', with an extra 'elbow' to direct the water straight into the engine's tank. It was lagged and supported for part of its height, controlled by a stop cock and key, and was protected by a light wooden fence.

There was a rather elementary loading gauge, with timber post, near the coaling stage, but some time during 1931 this was replaced by a new one, constructed mainly of two lengths of old rail.

There were never any signals on the railway, nor passing loops, since only one locomotive was in use, but there was telephonic communication with Alne. In the last years, however, this seems to have been out of use.

Turning now to the track itself, this was laid almost entirely as a surface line, since the route was practically level, and a stretch of 1 in 100 was the only real gradient. At Alne, the trackwork seems to have always been of chaired pattern, but soon after leaving the station it changed to 'Vignoles' flat-bottomed section, weighing 60 lb. to the yard, and this was used for the remainder of the railway for many years. Ballast consisted mainly of ashes, well packed, and the track was commendably free from weeds until the drastic reduction of staff after World War II made it impossible to maintain this standard.

By 1930, a small amount of chaired track was to be seen, e.g. near Alne level crossing, and parts of Easingwold yard, but most of the F.B. material remained until 1943/4, when Mr Coates wisely decided to re-lay the line throughout with second-hand bull head rail and chairs. This 'ploughing back' of war-time profits – to the tune of over £7,000 – was criticised by some shareholders, who would have preferred to receive some return on their investments; but it was, in fact, made in the interests of safety, for something like 60,000 tons of ammunition and war materials were moved over the Easingwold Railway during World War II. This track, although latterly a bit uneven, was pretty solid, and with 'outside' attention served until the closure. Two short lengths of the old F.B. track also survived to the end – the spur leading to the disused engine shed, and the outermost siding, near the steam wagon shed.

At one time, two platelayers were employed, under the charge of Mr Paragreen, Senr, but by 1947, when only four or five men worked the railway, there were no spare men for this job. Hence, track maintenance was carried out by LNER (and later BR) employees, two of whom, Mr Wilson, Senr and his son Maurice (of York MPD), did this in their spare time. This was mostly a week-end task, but urgent repairs would be attended to during the week, in the evenings.

Quite a presentable mixed train coming into Easingwold station in 1911 with the ex-North London brake bringing up the rear. *Locomotive Publishing Co.*

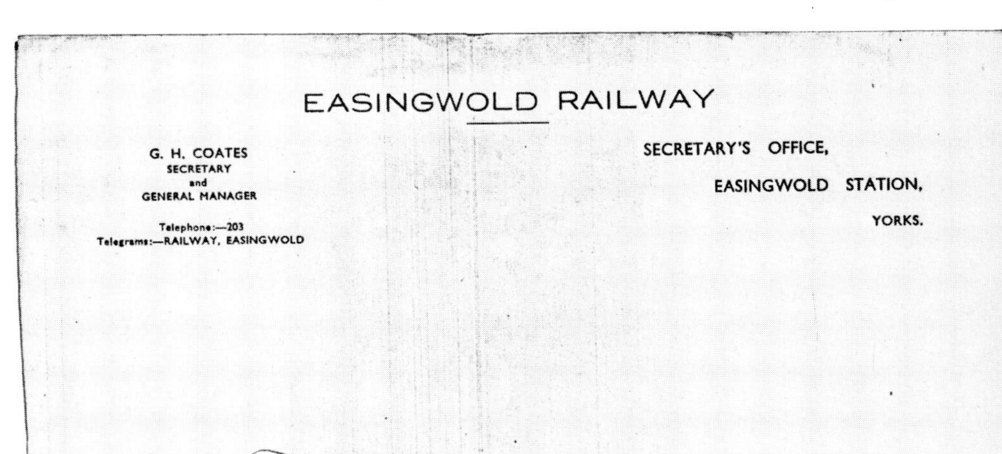

EASINGWOLD RAILWAY

G. H. COATES
SECRETARY
and
GENERAL MANAGER

Telephone:—203
Telegrams:—RAILWAY, EASINGWOLD

SECRETARY'S OFFICE,
EASINGWOLD STATION,
YORKS.

Locomotive No. 2 in the siding next to the main line at Alne. *Photomatic Ltd*

A well cleaned No. 2 awaits its next run bunker-first to Alne – a timeless and popular inter-war view. *S. Dewsbury (Oakwood Press)*

Hudswell Clarke & Co. Ltd, Works official photograph of the builders' standard 13″ cylinder 0–6–0 saddle similar to Easingwold No. 2 *Countess of Warwick*, Works No. 579 built 1901 for Desford Coal Co. Ltd, Desford, near Leicester.

R.N. Redman Collection

The three stalwarts of the Easingwold railway all in one view. Engine No. 2 with George Paragreen in the cab and Edward (Jack) Morse with hands on hip (c.1936).

Lens of Sutton

Chapter Three

Locomotives

Previous descriptions of the Easingwold Railway all appear to credit the line with only ever having owned two locomotives. This is not, however, the case. There were in fact three, but it is true to say the first only made a very brief appearance on the scene which probably accounts for the misunderstanding.

All three locomotives were products of the long established Leeds builders Hudswell Clarke & Co., of the Railway Foundry in the parish of Hunslet. First to enter service and used for the opening of the line was a typical industrial or contractors' four-coupled saddle tank named *Easingwold*, built to Hudswell's Works No. 342. Delivery was promised for 15th June, 1891, but in point of fact, it left South Leeds on 24th June. For this modest machine, which weighed only 12 tons 11 cwt. empty, the cash price would have been £720, but the railway entered into a hire purchase agreement with a cash deposit of £160 and 12 equal payments of £52, spread over a period of three years.

The basic specification of the locomotive was for an 0–4–0 saddle tank with 2 ft 9 in. diameter wheels and fitted with 10 in. diameter × 16 in. stroke outside cylinders set on a wheelbase of 5 ft 6 in. making it capable of negotiating a 35 ft radius curve. The working pressure was 130 lb./sq. in. Total heating surface was 273.6 sq. ft, with a grate area of 4.5 sq. ft. In full working order it weighed 15 tons 6 cwt. 1 qr. Details of the livery have not been recorded, but it seems highly probable that the finish was the maker's standard Midland red with a yellow or straw lining ¼ in. wide set 1 in. from the black edges, with the coupling rods red.

No official works photograph of 342 was taken and no shot in service has come to light. However, Hudswell Clarke recorded the locomotive as similar to 304/1888 *Hulme*, which was photographed prior to delivery to Thos. A. Walker for service on the Manchester Ship Canal construction contract. The only basic alterations to the Easingwold locomotive noted were the fitting of drop buffer beams, and thus the removing of the secondary block buffer and the fitting of guard irons and a screw jack.

The choice of this relatively tiny locomotive is still a mystery but it was probably a quick delivery and, more to the point, it was cheap. It must have become obvious very quickly that the engine was underpowered for the potential traffic and the hard work required of a railway with only one locomotive. On top of that there was the problem that the Board of Trade did not look kindly on the use of a four-wheeled locomotive in passenger service, and it was soon on its way back to the builders.

Despite its lack of success at Easingwold the locomotive went on to enjoy a brief, if rather rough, life and was virtually never out of work. Its first job was probably a short stint at Micklefield Colliery before being sold by Hudswell Clarke to the local Horsforth contractor Whitaker Bros on 7th November, 1891 for £670, and was delivered to Armley for use on their Great Northern Railway widening contract, where it carried Whitaker Bros No. 16.

The latter eventually sold it to Wakefield Coal & Lime in December, 1904, and later re-purchased it for a short period before trading it in to the builders

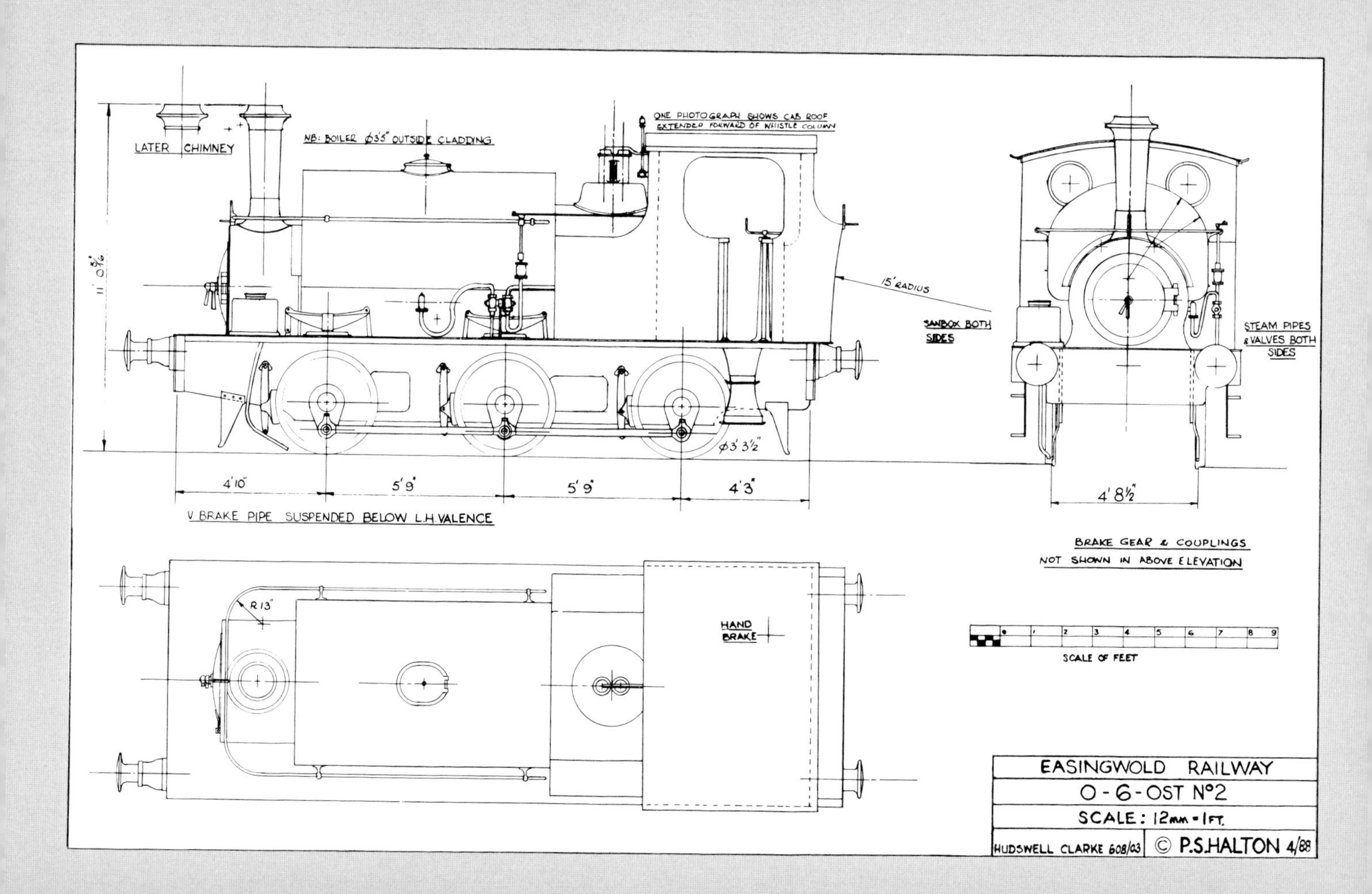
LATER CHIMNEY
NB: BOILER ϕ3'5" OUTSIDE CLADDING
ONE PHOTOGRAPH SHOWS CAB ROOF EXTENDED FORWARD OF WHISTLE COLUMN
11' 0⅝"
15' RADIUS
SANDBOX BOTH SIDES
STEAM PIPES & VALVES BOTH SIDES
ϕ3' 3½"
4'10"
5'9"
5'9"
4'3"
4' 8½"
V BRAKE PIPE SUSPENDED BELOW L.H. VALENCE
BRAKE GEAR & COUPLINGS NOT SHOWN IN ABOVE ELEVATION
R13"
HAND BRAKE
0 1 2 3 4 5 6 7 8 9
SCALE OF FEET
EASINGWOLD RAILWAY
0-6-0ST Nº2
SCALE: 12mm = 1FT.
HUDSWELL CLARKE 608/03
© P.S.HALTON 4/88

Works official photograph of Hudswell Clarke (No. 304 built 1888) *Hulme* built to the same design as the Easingwold Railway's first locomotive No. 342 built 1891.
R.N. Redman Collection

Hudswell Clarke 0–6–0ST (No. 257 built 1884) *Trent* photographed in service at Garforth, near Leeds.
R.N. Redman Collection

in February 1906, who soon hired it out to Glasshoughton & Castleford Colliery Ltd. They later purchased it on 14th March, 1908 for the princely sum of £300 plus the hire charges to date and ran it for another year before scrapping it. By industrial locomotive standards it had been a relatively short life, but a hard one!

On 21st July, four days prior to the official opening of the line, the Board placed an order with Hudswell Clarke for a six-coupled locomotive of increased power. To say the job was top priority must be an understatement for the new engine, to be named *Easingwold*, carried Works No. 334 and departed the Leeds works 30 days later on 20th August, 1891.

A typical contractor's design of the period it must have been yet again a standard design partially built to stock and capable of a quick delivery. Once again the railway shied away from a cash purchase price of £1,025 and settled for a deposit of £225 and 12 equal payments of £74 10s. 0*d*., spread over three years. Hudswell Clarke also noted they paid a 2½ per cent commission for the order to Mr Wood.

The basic specification for No. 334 was for a 12 ton (empty) 0–6–0 saddle tank with 3 ft diameter wheels and inside cylinders 12 in. in diameter × 18 in. stroke and designed to carry 10 cwt. of coal in the cab and 450 gallons of water in the saddle tank. Finished in Midland red (recorded as maroon) as the previous locomotive, this time it carried polished brass plates on the tank sides lettered *Easingwold*. The only departure from the standard design of the period was that the locomotive was to be fitted with one pump and one injector.

The new locomotive settled down to a regular routine and continued without major problems until early 1903 when a new firebox was required, whereupon the railway sold it out of service. It was shipped to York to the North Eastern locomotive works to be overhauled and a new firebox fitted, before being moved to the Ponteland Light Railway construction in Northumberland.

This NER branch constructed under a Light Railway Order was being built by J.C. Lant, a Newcastle-based contractor who took over the ownership of the locomotive. The Ponteland line is another interesting by-way; completed in 1905, it was intended to be electrified if the passenger traffic warranted it, but right up to the end in June 1929 it was worked by a 'steam autocar'.

Easingwold was observed being used on the construction of Sculcoates (Hull) station *c*.1905, before it passed into the hands of the Ministry of Munitions at the Coprolite Works, at Trumpington, a site which lasted until *c*.1923/24. No. 334 must have been disposed of prior to closure as a note in the old Hudswell order book records the locomotive with Murchen MacDonald & Wilson in 1922. Its subsequent history, if any, has been lost.

Easingwold's third, and last, locomotive proved to be the mainstay of the line for over 40 years, inevitably known by the locals as 'The Coffee Pot'. Built to Hudswell Clarke Works No. 608, following an order dated 27th April, 1903, this was practically another engine 'off the shelf' as delivery was executed by 7th May, an astonishing 10 days. This time, the choice was a 20 ton 'standard' 13″ six-coupled design built in quantities over the years for industrial lines and contractors. Yet again cost was paramount in the company's mind, and the builder's offer of £1,185 cash was rejected in favour of a deposit of £500 with £385 in September 1903, and £300 in March 1904. The other offer was less attractive, that of £500 down and £685 in March 1904, with £20 interest.

By Easingwold standards their 'No. 2', (HC 608) was quite a powerful machine, a six-coupled saddle tank weighing 24 tons 15 cwt. in working order. It had a wheel base of 11 ft 6 in. with 3 ft 3½ in. driving wheels and inside cylinder 13 in. diameter by 20 in. stroke. The boiler pressure was 160 lb. sq. in., total heating surface 454 sq. ft, with a grate area of 8.43 sq. ft. Coal capacity was 1 ton and 550 gallons of water were carried. Both steam and hand brakes operated on all wheels and steam heating equipment was fitted for winter passenger service.

The couplings were of loose 3-link type. The domeless boiler was fed by two injectors, and had the Ramsbottom-type safety valves set to 150/160 lb. p.s.i. Twin gauge glasses were fitted.

The frames had a length of 20 ft 7 in., and the timber buffer beams were faced with steel plate. Width over footplating was 7 ft 6 in. (over cab roof, 7 ft 8 in.), and height from rail to top of chimney, just over 11 ft.

Like the previous locomotives, it was built for right hand drive, and a useful addition, fitted at some date unknown, was an 'outrigger' regulator handle, clamped to, and extending to the right of, the normal centrally-mounted control, thus enabling the driver easily to operate the regulator whilst leaning out of the cab during shunting operations. Other useful extras were hinged doors to both cab entrances, and there were also no less than four seats – all plain wooden ones, however!

When delivered, this locomotive, which was not named but merely designated 'No. 2', was painted in the same style as *Easingwold* – in what her driver for many years, Mr George Paragreen, described as 'Midland Red'. Apparently there was a time lapse between the departure of the older 0–6–0ST and the arrival of 'No. 2', and the general similarity of design, and livery, of the two engines was such as to cause two young lads – Mr George Paragreen and his brother – some confusion. One vowed that the locomotive was indeed a new one, whilst the other was equally certain it was *Easingwold* back again – '. . . and so they had a fight to settle it!' At any rate, this little story should effectively contradict the information, which has occasionally turned-up in print, that Easingwold engines were painted green!

'No. 2' was returned to Hudswell Clarke's for overhaul, during the summer of 1911, and an old NER six-coupled tender locomotive, No. 1263, built by Hopkins, Gilkes & Co., worked the traffic for some time. This was evidently the date when 'No. 2' first acquired her long-familiar black livery, relieved by a single red line. The coupling rods, as well as the buffer cases and buffer beams were vermilion, and the tank sides bore the inscription 'Easingwold Rly. Co. No. 2' in gilt letters, shaded red. With the addition of well-polished brass and copper fittings, the result was decidedly pleasing, for the little engine was always kept in clean condition.

In September 1924, the engine was sent to the makers for re-building. On this occasion, an elderly 0–6–0ST was loaned to the company by Hudswell Clarke's. This engine, named *Trent*, had outside cylinders, and an elementary 'wrap-over' cab, without side sheets, and was painted maroon. The maker's number and date are believed to be 257/'84, and the locomotive went new to the Trent Iron Co., of Scunthorpe. It is known that at some time prior to 1924 the engine worked for a time at the Garforth Collieries, near Leeds, and a photograph in the McDougall Collection, in York Railway Museum, depicts her there. She later became No. 87 in McAlpine's stock. At Easingwold, however, *Trent* showed a tendency to run a hot axle-box, and certainly was not so well liked as 'No. 2'. The latter duly returned to the railway as good as new, again repainted black, and with her maker's plate endorsed 'Rebuilt 1924'. Little outward difference was discernible, apart from some alteration to the feed water pipework.

Once again, in the early 1930s, 'No. 2' journeyed to Leeds for overhaul, and plating of the firebox sides, and this time, she came back painted in maroon, lined in yellow and vermilion. This was her last major overhaul, as it later turned out. During World War II, a great deal of extra traffic, which included many thousands of tons of war material, passed over the railway, and by 1946, the strain was beginning to tell on the little 'Hudswell'.

A visit on 8th June, 1946 coincided with the 'Victory Celebrations' and 'No. 2' had been given a day off. Ken Hartley recorded it standing in the shed with all its 'bright work' polished, and its maroon paint having mellowed to a dark mahogany shade. Sadly it was all top show, the locomotive's 'Indian Summer' would soon be over, for in 1947 she was sent to Darlington requiring a new boiler and firebox, and other repairs. Throughout 1947 and most of 1948, she lay in the North Road Works yard in very forlorn condition, with look-out glasses broken and 'Easingwold' painted out from the title on her saddle tank. Eventually, in the winter of 1948–49, she was broken up, in the scrap yard, by a private firm. One of her maker's plates can be seen in York Railway Museum, and the injector handwheels were for many years in the possession of the late Mr 'Jack' Morse, who was one of her old drivers.

The cost of the repairs to 'No. 2' found necessary by the Darlington Mechanical Engineer was estimated at £1,400, and he advised that a good second-hand engine would be preferable. He recommended such an engine, a 13 in. Hudswell Clarke, be obtained from Sir Lindsay Parkinson & Co., Ltd, at a price of £3,500. In the end, however, this deal was not concluded.

Early in 1947 Mr Coates, together with his wife, went to Hudswell Clarke's works to discuss the possibility of the purchase of another engine. The one they inspected was Works No. 1682, *Julia* built originally in 1937 to basically the same design as their old 'No. 2'. It had been rebuilt by the makers after working for Sir Lindsay Parkinson & Co. Ltd, of Blackpool on the Euxton Munitions Factory at Chorley, Lancs. The original cost was £1,700, but it was now on the market for £4,000, a figure out of reach of the Easingwold line's slim resources and it eventually left the works in June 1947, for the British Sugar Corporation at Newark.

Since the departure from Easingwold of 'No. 2', motive power was hired from the LNER, and subsequently BR, and indeed this arrangement continued, perforce, until the railway closed in 1957. It was, however, a very heavy drain on the Easingwold Railway Co's resources; at one period, the charge was £40 5*s.* 0*d.* per week. The financial aspect will be dealt with in a later chapter, while the motive power itself is here detailed. The locomotive supplied, from York Shed, was, during the last decade of operation, always an 0–6–0T, of either class 'J71' or 'J72', of varying antiquity but of consistently sombre appearance, due to lack of cleaning. Nevertheless, some of these engines were not bad mechanically, although their external condition left a lot to be desired; their condition could be partially due to the fact they were too tall to fit in the engine shed and had to 'sleep rough', outside in all weathers.

The following engines have been noted by Ken Hartley at various times: *class 'J71'* – BR 8281 (Darlington 1140/'92), 'E.8310', 8246, 68253, 68273 (built 1891), and 8297. *Class 'J72'*: Nos 68677, 68699 (Darlington 1914), and 68698 (which was the last engine in use).

At various earlier times motive power was supplied by the NER and later LNER, as for example in 1923, when No. 1140 put in a few days there during December. On another occasion, a class 'H' ('Y7') 0–4–0T was sent along, but apparently the BoT objection, mentioned previously, still held good, and it is understood that the four-wheeler was replaced by the class 'H2' 0–6–0T No. 407, which had also worked on the Selby–Cawood branch (the one-time 'Cawood, Wistow and Selby Lt Rly'), and the North Sunderland Railway.

So far as can now be ascertained, no other ex-NER types or classes worked on the Easingwold Railway, and no diesel ever passed over its track.

Locomotive No. 1 *Easingwold* and original train in Easingwold station, photographed pre-1903. *Mrs M. Coates Collection*

The last Easingwold Railway coach stored for preservation at Cliffe Common on the Derwent Valley Light Railway, 18th May, 1959. *K.E. Hartley*

Detail of the lettering on van No. E70221E on loan to the Easingwold Light Railway. *R.M. Casserley*

Chapter Four

Rolling Stock

The first coaches used on the railway were two ancient four-wheelers obtained from the NER, but nothing is known of their earlier history. They were approximately 26 ft in length, and had low, almost flat, roofs, with luggage-rails on top, and a series of eyelets along the edges – fittings which emphasised the antiquity of these vehicles. Coach No. 1 had four compartments, of which the centre pair were more spacious than the end ones, and had obviously once been of a superior class. The other carriage – No. 2 – was similar, except that in place of one of the end compartments, there was a tiny Guard's/Luggage section, with small, box-like, look-outs. No lamps are visible in the only known photographs, nor are any details available as to livery, but 'Second' class indications, in full, appear on the doors, at the waist-line, and the lower panel of each door carried a decorative scroll, lettered 'E.R.' These vehicles were replaced about 1903, and were set up on struts, to serve as a store for the goods traffic, and continued in use for very many years. They were certainly there in 1931, but probably disappeared shortly before, or during, World War II.

Their replacements consisted of three ex-North London Railway four-wheelers, two of which were composites, with two first class and three second class compartments. The partitions in the latter reached only up to the top of the seats, and one 'quarter light' served adjacent compartments. They had a length of approximately 28 ft, and were fitted with oil lamps. An old photograph – probably taken around 1903 – shows that the class indications were made in full, 'First' and 'Second', on raised boards just beneath the door windows. A rather later view reveals that this style had been replaced by numerals on the raised discs on the door lower panels, by which time, also, one coach – and possibly both – had had a first class compartment demoted to 'second'. It is interesting to note that the Easingwold was many years ahead of the times in adopting the more logical designations of 'First' and 'Second', and apparently never had any 'Third' class.

The third NLR vehicle was a Guard's and Luggage van, with a raised 'Bird Cage' look-out at one end. These three coaches were finished in brown, with the class indications painted in yellow, and while the standard of comfort may have been an improvement on that of the original stock, it was – in 1918, at any rate – a long way below that offered on the NER!

Round about 1920, the NLR vehicles were taken out of running. The van body was placed near the siding, at Crankley level crossing, and used as a shed for some years, and one of the composites, less running gear, was placed at the lineside, just at the rear of the engine shed, where it remained, in ever-worsening condition, until 1953, when it was finally broken up, and used for 'lighting-up'. The fate of the other composite is not known.

The next coaching stock came from the NER, and consisted of two standard six-wheelers, with spoked wheels. For use of the Easingwold Railway, however, the middle axles, etc., were removed, and the vehicles were painted a medium brown, unlined, with the 'class' numerals, and initials 'E.R.', in yellow characters. Roofs were grey, and running gear the usual black finish. Approximate body dimensions were: length 32 ft, width

It would be impossible to improve on the cleanliness of the coach – 30th June, 1933.
H.C. Casserley

The last year of passenger service in 1948 saw the ex-Great Central 1st and 2nd coach getting very scruffy. Internally, only the 1st class was fit to travel in, but soon that would only be required for parcel traffic.
R.N. Redman

8 ft, and height 7 ft. One coach had five compartments, all second class, while the other was a Brake Composite, with one first class and two second class compartments. They were certainly in use late in 1930, but during the next 12 months they had been replaced by a single first and second class Brake Composite (6-wh. 'Brake Third' No. 2442, purchased 8.3.1930, but not in use until the end of the year) similar to the previous one – the only noticeable differences being the retention of the centre pair of wheels – spoked – and the title 'Easingwold Railway', which appeared on the waist panels, in place of the initials 'E.R.' At some later date, however, the middle axle was taken out, as is evident from photographs taken in 1937. This solitary vehicle was probably ample for the passenger traffic still remaining in the later 1930s, and seems to have remained on the line until about 1946, when it was replaced by the last coach actually owned by the company.

This, again, was a 6-wheel, first and second class Brake Composite, offering the same accommodation as the previous ones, and having the same livery, although the full title on the waist panels had given place to the earlier 'E.R.' This coach was an ex-GCR vehicle, of about 1906, acquired, it is understood, from the Cheshire Lines Committee, and was very similar to the earlier NER Brake Composites, except that it had Mansell wheels, and the guards' 'look-outs' were at the end of the body.

By 1948 it had become somewhat dilapidated with very faded paintwork and badly torn upholstery; the first class just about fit to travel in and second class barely acceptable for storing parcels, but since the passenger service ceased at the end of November in that year, this was perhaps of little moment, and the old vehicle continued in use, for parcels traffic, until sometime in 1956, when it was replaced by a vehicle borrowed from BR. This was a high-roofed, ex-LNER, 35 ft, 4-wheel Passenger Luggage Van of 5 tons capacity, No. E70221E, in standard maroon, and was lettered in yellow, at the right hand bottom corner of the body, 'On loan to the Easingwold Light Rly'.

The old ex-Great Central Railway brake composite coach was purchased early in 1957 by Mr J.H. Bowes for private preservation, and was soon moved to the Cliffe Common terminus of the 16 miles-long Derwent Valley Light Railway. There it stayed in a storage siding at the junction with the Selby Market Weighton line until the threatened closure of the DVLR in 1965 necessitated the movement down the line to Elvington station. A siding by the level crossing was home until the Railway Preservation Society acquired it, together with the old 6-wheel 'Birdcage' van of the DVLR. The pair of antique vehicles were moved by low loader in December 1968 to the Chasewater Light Railway at Brownhills, West Midlands.

Superb restoration of the former Easingwold coach to GE condition was well advanced when mindless vandals struck and set the coach on fire. Fortunately, the fire was contained to the brake end, although about 40 per cent of the coach was subsequently damaged. Thankfully, the Transport Trust came forward with a grant, and restoration started again on this important relic.

This concludes the description of Easingwold Railway rolling stock, for the line never possessed any goods wagons of its own, any such requirements having always been supplied by the old NER, and its successors.

EASINGWOLD RAILWAY

EVERY
SATURDAY
UNTIL FURTHER NOTICE,

CHEAP
Third-Class Return Tickets to

YORK
Fare - - 1/11,

Will be issued by the

a.m. 10-15, a.m. 11-15, p.m. 1-20 and p.m. 5-0, Trains.

A LATE TRAIN LEAVES YORK AT 10-57 p.m.
FOR EASINGWOLD.

Chapter Five

Services and Operation

In the earlier days of the Easingwold Railway, and up to the years of World War One, there was a passenger service of nine trains daily, in each direction, on weekdays only – there has never been a Sunday service on the line.

The April 1900 edition of *Bradshaw* gives the following details:

	am	am	am	am	pm	pm	pm	pm	pm
Easingwold, dep.	7.43	8.40	10.15	11.30	1.37	3.00	5.02	6.38	8.10
Alne, arr.	7.51	8.48	10.23	11.38	1.45	3.08	5.10	6.46	8.18

	am	am	am	pm	pm	pm	pm	pm	pm
Alne, dep.	8.10	9.12	10.45	12.32	1.52	3.18	5.38	7.12	8.29
Easingwold, arr.	8.18	9.20	10.53	12.40	2.00	3.26	5.46	7.20	8.37

It seems likely that these times would not greatly vary from the original timetables, until World War I, but the NER timetable for July 1915 showed the 6.38 pm had been withdrawn, and the last train re-timed to leave Easingwold at 7.51 pm.

By 1921, or earlier, the last departure from Easingwold was at 6.45 pm, and the service of eight trains continued as below:

	am	am	am	am	pm	pm	pm	pm
Easingwold, dep.	7.36	8.34	10.15	11.15	1.20	3.15	5.00	6.45
Alne, arr.	7.44	8.42	10.23	11.23	1.28	3.23	5.08	6.53

	am	am	am	pm	pm	pm	pm	pm
Alne, dep.	8.10	9.06	10.40	12.37	1.38	3.37	5.45	7.18
Easingwold, arr.	8.18	9.14	10.48	12.45	1.46	3.45	5.53	7.26

until 1927, when the 10.15 am and 6.45 pm were withdrawn. This six-train service operated, with only slight alterations, until May 1931, when an additional train at 10.25 am was added:

	am	am	am *	am	pm	pm	pm
Easingwold, dep.	7.30	8.36	10.25	11.02	1.15	3.15	5.00
Alne, arr.	7.38	8.44	10.33	11.10	1.23	3.23	5.08

	am	am	am	am	pm	pm	pm
Alne, dep.	8.10	9.02	10.40	11.20	1.38	3.37	5.47
Easingwold, arr.	8.18	9.10	10.48	11.28	1.46	3.45	5.55

* On Saturdays leaves at 10.10 am.

This seven-train service continued, with minor variations, until 30th April, 1939, but from 1st May two trains (12.45 pm and 3.0 pm) became 'Saturdays Only', and early in December war-time alterations cut them out altogether.

The classic light railway train; locomotive No. 2 and single coach alongside Easingwold station platform. The flat bottomed rail and lack of ballast show up well in this undated view. *Lens of Sutton*

NER class 'J71' No. 8282, on hire, pauses by the water crane at Easingwold on 9th September, 1947, with the coach in a very rough state.
H.M. Livesey (R.C. Riley Collection)

British Rail (ex-LNER) class 'J72' 0–6–0T No. 68677 returning with the Saturday am 'Goods' from Alne on 13th August, 1949, passing the engine shed – only one cattle truck forms the load. *K.E. Hartley*

Still doing quite good business, class 'J72' locomotive No. 68699 arrives at Easingwold with a long freight on 22nd May, 1954. *E.G. Cope*

An attractive but undated view of locomotive No. 2 arriving at Easingwold yard with a fair sized mixed train. A well loaded private owner's coal wagon is parked on the goods siding behind. *Lens of Sutton*

The Railway's Secretary and Manager G.H. Coates surveys the afternoon train in Easingwold station – Summer 1930. The previous winter must have been a bad one as the locomotive has been fitted with home made cab side doors. *K.E. Hartley*

An immaculate turnout; locomotive No. 2 and its coach ready to depart from Easingwold on 30th June, 1933. *H.C. Casserley*

The same train, viewed from the other side. *H.C. Casserley*

From 1st April, 1940, the service was reduced to three trains each way; but the 12.45 'Saturdays Only' was restored, and continued to run until 6th October, 1946.

The October 1946 timetable revealed a further cut, to only two return trips daily, with departures from Easingwold at 8.08 am and 5 pm, but there was an additional Saturday departure from Easingwold at 1 pm.

On 21st May, 1948, the 5 pm ceased to run on Saturdays, and the passenger service was finally withdrawn altogether on 29th November of that year.

The normal journey time was eight minutes, but this was liable to be somewhat exceeded with a heavy 'mixed' train.

It appears that from the opening of the line, until the end of 1893, third class tickets were issued on all trains, but a notice in *The Easingwold Advertiser* for 30th December, 1893, announced that these would henceforth be discontinued, except on the first and last trains of the day, and this practice seems to have been in vogue until at least 1917 – and perhaps later. The third class travellers had to use second class accommodation, of course, since no third class coaches were in use. In the latter part of 1924, Cheap Day Return third class fares to York were introduced, available 'every Saturday until further notice', on the 10.15, 11.15 am, 1.20 and 5pm trains, the fare being 1*s.* 11*d.* There was a late train (for some of the period at least, this was a rail motor bus) which left York at 10.57 pm and the connecting Easingwold Railway train left Alne at 11.20 pm. (The '10.57 pm ex-York' appears in LNER timetables from 22.9.1924 to 30.4.1928.)

Passenger receipts for 1947 brought in only £18 0*s.* 8*d.* (of which the 8*d.* was paid by the sole first class passenger!); 635 second class passengers were carried during the year. An average of roughly two passengers per day indicates how this traffic had fallen away.

Apart from the Cheap Day Returns to York, just mentioned, in years gone by excursions direct from Easingwold had been run to places as far afield as Liverpool, and for some years there was a 'Special' from Leeds to Easingwold, on 'Show Day'. Even in the 1930s excursions were occasionally made to Scarborough, one of the last being 21st July, 1937, and it is recalled that after one of the seaside specials, 'No. 2' had some difficulty in bringing the six LNER bogie coaches up the 1 in 100 bank from Alne.

Regular travellers in the 1930s were the Alne children who attended school in Easingwold. Mr Harry M. Pattison still recalls those halcyon days when he was a pupil at Easingwold Grammar School.

If the weather was good he made the journey by cycle, but in winter he went by train ('the coffee pot'). Half a dozen boys and the same number of girls travelled in separate compartments. New boys had a rough ride being 'put under the belt', which took the form of beating with the window strap. The train travelled very slowly and if the level crossing gates were not open, the train had to stop whilst the fireman climbed down to open and close them. If the driver saw someone had missed the train, it was regular practice to reverse back and pick them up. There was a slot machine on the station where for one old penny you could buy a cigarette and two matches in a packet – very useful for the schoolboys! His recollections close with, 'By road was one mile further than by train from Alne to Easingwold. I could beat it on the cycle if I really tried'.

Details of fares, at any rate in the early days, are not available, but in 1917 the single fares were 6*d*., 4*d*., and 3*d*., respectively for 1st, 2nd and 3rd class. For many years these prices remained unchanged for the 1st and 2nd classes ('Third' fares had been discontinued altogether, sometime after World War I) but after the Second War, the charges were increased to 8*d*. and 6*d*. (2nd Cl. Return cost 1*s*.). A rather unusual ticket was 'Available for 3 days, including day of issue' – a '2nd Cl. Single', Easingwold to Alne, costing 7½*d*., and a similar ticket for a 'Child' was 4*d*. The date of these is unknown.

Season or 'Contract' Tickets were also issued by the railway – a '3 months', dated 9.9.1914–8.12.1914, for a 'Scholar' cost 5*s*., while a '12 months' Contract, endorsed 'Fridays and Show Day' cost 15*s*. Strangely, in neither case is the class specified.

The ordinary tickets were similar in pattern to the LNER standard Thomas Edmondson cards (30.5 mm × 57 mm), basically in a rather pale green (with a different colour for specials). On the reverse side they carried the note 'Not transferable, issued subject to the Bye-Laws, Regulations, Notices and Conditions published in the Company's Bills & Notices'.

Through bookings were available to 12 'North Eastern' stations, chief of which were Harrogate, Leeds, Scarborough, Stockton, and York. For destinations other than the select 12, passengers had to re-book at Alne station.

After regular passenger services ceased, at least three 'Specials' were run, in the 1950s. The first of these, on 28th September, 1951, was put on for the 'York Miniature Railway Society', and consisted of an ex-NER 0–6–0T, the aged ex-GCR coach, and an open wagon – most of the party appear to have preferred the latter accommodation, for the coach had by now become very 'tatty'. This trip, with the engine carrying a special headboard, was something of a festive occasion, and received due attention from local newspapers, some of which called it a 'Sentimental Journey' – with Laurence Sterne in mind, no doubt.

In 1957, with final closure looming up, there were two notable special trains over the Easingwold Railway organised as part of longer railtours. The first named 'The Yorkshire Man' started in York at 12.30 pm on Sunday 2nd June and embraced 150 miles of rail travel, organised by the Branch Line Society. The first job was to get all attending to sign over a sixpenny stamp on a form indemnifying the Easingwold Railway Company from any claim in case of an accident.

BR 0–6–0 No. 68726 in the hands of driver Paragreen hauled the eight open wagons used, together with the four-wheel passenger luggage van on loan from British Railways. As the train left Alne, two fog detonators were set off, startling cows in a nearby field. An article by Bill Lang in the *Yorkshire Life Illustrated* of August 1957 was entitled 'Easingwold did us proud'. His journalistic prose recorded:

> We grabbed the sides of the wagons and held on, as with bits of soot flying back into our faces, we made the journey into the unknown. In fact, with the high green walls of foliage around, it seemed rather like a journey into some mysterious South

> American jungle on a single track line. The difference was that when we ran up the bank into Easingwold Station we got a real Yorkshire welcome, as half the township turned out to greet us.

He later recorded 'On the special Sunday of which I wrote, the old-fashioned booking hall on Easingwold station was open and Mr L. Jackson, a relief station master (BR) from the Helmsley district, was busy selling sets of the line's old passenger tickets at 2*s.* 6*d.*'

The second special came three weeks later when the little line was host to the Railway Correspondence & Travel Society on Sunday 23rd June. This run attracted around 300 passengers and required 10 open wagons and the usual van, this time hauled by 'J71' No. 68246.

It may be that the bad state of the old GCR Brake Composite, was one reason for abandoning the passenger service, but this vehicle continued in use on the goods and parcels trains just as it had previously done, and there were still two return workings daily to Alne. In 1954 – and probably for some years previous – the morning train on Mondays and Saturdays left Easingwold at 8.20 am, but from Tuesdays to Fridays inclusive the departure time was 7.25 am. In the early part of 1956, the Saturday train was discontinued, and in the last year, there was just one regular train at 7.25 am, with other workings 'as required'.

Prior to 1948, goods traffic was normally attached to the scheduled passenger trains, although not all of these ran as 'Mixed' – indeed, most of Ken Hartley's journeys were made on purely passenger trains.

The first recorded goods traffic was a batch of horses destined for Malton 'Show' in July, 1897; the very last load was several wagons of sugar beet, on Friday 27th December, 1957. In the intervening 66 years, the railway carried probably all the anticipated types of traffic – not all, perhaps, in the quantities so optimistically expected back in 1887 – and during World War II, at least, large tonnages of ammunition and war materials – which certainly had not been envisaged.

For local delivery of parcels traffic, the Easingwold Railway for very many years owned a 4-wheel dray, or rulley, but a local carter actually provided the horse, and did the delivering and collecting. For a considerable number of years, prior to his death in 1920, a Mr Brownlow had performed this service. He was succeeded in the job by Mr Ernest Ward, who carried on until the line closed in 1957 and, with his grey mare 'Andy', was a familiar sight in the district.

The steam wagon road services of the North Eastern Railway prior to World War I are an interesting and little recorded sideline of railway history. The always progressive NER had introduced petrol buses as early as 1903, but two years later turned to steam for its road wagon fleet mainly to serve outlying farms in the Vale of York. By 1906 they had built up a collection of 17 exotic, if not totally reliable, vehicles from no less than five different manufacturers, namely, The Seaham Harbour Engine Works, who produced the Londonderry steam wagon, The Straker Steam Vehicle Co. Ltd, of Bristol, The St Pancras Iron Works, London, Coulthard & Co., Preston, and the Thornycroft Steam Wagon Co. Ltd.

The poor country roads of the period inevitably added to the unreliability of the wagons and costs in spares alone caused problems over the few years they were employed. The NER commenced its pioneer service in October 1904 with regular deliveries and collections between Tollerton (the next station to Alne) and Brandsby. This was rather a blow to the Easingwold Railway with the inevitable loss of revenue due to reduced traffic, and they lost no time in complaining to the main line company. The NER the next year undertook to move its railhead to Easingwold, in an agreement made on 24th November, 1905 for the two companies to partake in a joint venture in providing a wagon service between the railway terminus and the villages of Brandsby, Crayke and Stillington.

The North Eastern Railway was to provide two wagons and crews and the Easingwold Railway staff had to do the loading and unloading at Easingwold station. The light railway had to provide yard space and station accommodation as required and any appliances as were needed, as well as undertaking to build at its own cost a suitable shed with a pit, to garage and service the two wagons. The design of this had to be approved by the NER. On the financial side, the Easingwold Railway had to keep all the accounts of incoming and outgoing deliveries in return for a 50 per cent stake in any revenue which might accrue.

The service to Brandsby commenced on 1st March, 1906, but the volume of business never reached the amount anticipated and it was not a very profitable venture. Nevertheless it lasted until September 1915. The first wagon used from Easingwold was almost certainly a vertical boilered Straker steamer, running on steel tyred wheels and having an undertype engine beneath the cab and wagon body. Later a Londonderry was used of a very similar design. All the types bore a similar general appearance to the more famous Sentinel type and local people recall them as such, but in point of fact the NER never possessed any of that particular make.

Between the wars the steam wagon shed was used by a private road haulier called Artillery Transport Co. They owned two open cab 'Vulcan' petrol wagons which carried the initials 'A.T.L.' and lasted until about 1925, having been fully employed for a time on moving fabricated sections of pylons for the erection of a length of the Thirsk to Malton power line. One driver involved with the company at the end was a local man, Bill Bisby, who also undertook the maintenance of the two wagons. The shed was demolished and the pit filled in when the railway closed.

The Auction Mart, at the rear of the station, has already been mentioned, in Chapter Two, as being one of the company's assets, and the two level crossing keepers' cottages, of course, also belonged to the railway. There was, in addition, a row of four attractive brick dwellings known as 'Railway' or 'Station Cottages' which faced on to the Raskelf Road, near the goods yard entrance. These were occupied by railway employees for a weekly rent of 2*s*. 6*d*. deducted from their wages. After closure of the line they were sold for a nominal sum to the sitting tenants. Driver Jack Danby lived at No. 1, before the Paragreen family; Alf Franklin who looked after the station coalyard was in No. 2; Jack Morse and his family were the longest occupants spanning 55 years in No. 3; and porter/loader Mr Mason had No. 4.

The Easingwold Company at one time did a certain amount of shunting for the NER, at Alne, and for this received the sum of £10 per annum. This was, of course, more than offset by the charge made for the part-use of Alne station, which amounted to £30 a year – a figure which subsequently rose to £60, in a matter of four years.

The Easingwold Railway, of course, had its minor derailments, especially in the later years, and when 6-wheel coaches were in use, but, luckily, with little harm to life or property. So far as can be discovered, the line was equally fortunate as to accidents involving life, although, tragically, a boy named Gill was killed during shunting operations at Easingwold, in the early 1900s, and in 1908 a man named Ward lost a leg, at Alne. Another incident, which could easily have had serious results, occurred in August 1906, when four boys set some wagons in motion on a siding in Easingwold yard. They crashed through the level crossing gates at Crankley, and did not finally come to a stop until near Alne Station. Fortunately, nobody was hurt as a result of this foolish prank.

Crankley Crossing was the scene of another incident in 1909 when engine No. 2 with Danby and Lawson on the footplate collided with Billy Paragreen's donkey, fortunately with no ill effects to either party.

It may here be mentioned that the track was often used, when services had ceased for the day, as a footpath by local folk desiring to get from Alne to Easingwold by the shortest route – for example to visit the cinema at the latter place.

Stoppages of services, due to causes outside the company's control, were also extremely rare, and indeed Mr Morse could recall but one occasion, when in 1916–17 the line was blocked for two days with snow and ice, and all trains had to be cancelled. The national rail strike of 1955 caused some Easingwold Railway trains not to run, but the local staff duly reported for duty, and whenever there was a chance of making a connection at Alne, would light-up the old 0–6–0T and take a train along to the junction. In between these 'outings', they devoted their energies to weeding and generally making the track and yard at Easingwold look very tidy and well cared for.

Taken as a whole, up till about 1946 the railway seems to have managed to 'make ends meet' fairly comfortably, although this must not be taken to mean that it paid regular dividends throughout this period. It did not. The first year's gross revenue of £1,296 did not, in fact, cover expenses, but a letter from the General Manager of the NER to the promoters of the Cawood Railway, dated 4th July, 1894, stated that ' . . . the Easingwold Railway . . . receipts in 1893 were £1,409, and expenses £1,092'. A statement made by Henry Liversedge, Esq. regarding the Cawood line, in 1896, also referred to the Easingwold Railway ' . . . which pays, on 10,000 tons of goods traffic, and a steady flow of passengers'.

Things continued to improve, and in 1910 a clear profit of £767 was recorded, which enabled a 4 per cent dividend to be declared, and £315 to be carried forward. For a number of years a 3 per cent or 4 per cent dividend was paid, but after the mid-1920s road competition began to affect railway traffic generally, and the Easingwold shareholders received less interest. In 1931, only 1 per cent was paid, with none at all in the next decade. The heavy wartime traffic, however, brought a spell of prosperity to the little railway, and in 1943 a payment of 3 per cent was made.

No doubt the years 1944–5 would have given an even larger return, but, as stated earlier, for reasons of safety it was decided to renew the track completely, and thus there were no dividend payments.

Economy, in both construction and operation, was one of the objectives of the promoters of the Easingwold Railway. As the years went by, this policy had to be observed closely, with savings being effected wherever possible, and it seems likely that the company's application, in the late 1920s, to work the line as a Light Railway was made with the idea of securing some operational economies. Accordingly, early in 1928, the Minister of Transport made the following Order:

> 'The Easingwold Light Railway: Order, 1928', authorising the working of the Easingwold Railway; as a Light Railway under the Light Railways Acts, 1896 and 1912, as amended by the Railways Act, 1921.

Locomotive No. 2 with the full range of North London coaches. Note the hand lamp on the corner of the locomotive bunker. At the back one of the early NE coach bodies has been mounted on posts to be used as a store. *Locomotive Publishing Co.*

The end of the line – George Paragreen stands next to BR class 'J72' 0–6–0T No. 68698 shortly before leaving with the last train on Friday 27th December, 1957. *C.R. Evers*

The Branch Line Special parting the long grass on its way to Easingwold, 2nd June, 1957. *R.M. Casserley*

Chapter Six

The Last Decade

The end of the War caused a big drop in the W.D. traffic, and with other traffic also falling off, the railway began to lose money – the returns for 1947 reveal a debit balance of £1,078. Matters were not improved by the need to hire motive power from the LNER, and on 6th June, 1947, Mr Coates wrote to the Ministry of Transport to try and obtain some financial aid, suggesting either a loan at low interest, to buy a 'new' locomotive, or a grant, based on traffics, to cover increased operating costs, or a grant towards the hire of the LNER locomotive, pending a decision as to whether the Easingwold would be taken over by the BTC.

He pointed out that, during the War, the whole line had been relaid, because of the heavy W.D. traffic. This had cost £7,590, and a further £850 had been spent during 1943/4 on the repair and renovation of buildings. Furthermore, rates and charges had not increased in proportion to increased expenditure. He also said that the W.D. traffic had virtually ceased by the end of 1946, and the company was losing money. The £604 cash in hand, on 31st December, 1946, had by 31st May, 1947 shrunk to £395 – against which the LNER required £367 10s. 0*d*. for locomotive hire to 19th April, 1947, at £26 5s. 0*d*. per week. This was to continue until 'E.R. No. 2' was replaced.

The Ministry duly informed the BTC about all this, but both agreed that no help could be given. Bad luck indeed!

Traffic continued to fall during 1947 and, despite economies, so did receipts. There was by now a staff of only four or five men to work the line. The trend continued during 1948, and Mr Coates' appeals to the BTC for a reduction in the locomotive hire charges (then amounting to £40 5s. 0*d*. per week) did not bring the desired response. In November 1948, ill-health forced him to abandon his efforts to keep the railway solvent, and he retired from office.

Mr Arthur Caygill, the station master for many years, carried on the running of the line, *pro tem*., with a staff of four. At the time of the nationalisation of the railways on 1st January, 1948, he claimed to be the world's oldest railway man, a sprightly 76, with 50 years' service behind him, having originally been in the NER booking office at Alne.

On the run-up to the nationalisation of the 'Big Four', the newspapers speculated on the future of the Easingwold Railway and questioned if it would be caught in the net. This was best summed up by the regular train guard Joseph Parling, who was quoted as saying, 'the only regular passengers are three clerks employed by the LNER in York, but we don't get any revenue from them, because they travel free as servants of another railway company'.

1949 had been a better year for the railway, and the deficit carried forward to 1950 showed a reduction of £1,062 on the previous year. Traffic had included 736 tons of military equipment. This improved trend continued in the early part of 1950, apparently, and a meeting of shareholders, held on 1st June, at the station office, decided to carry on operating the railway. Following the retirement of Mr Coates, Mr H.F. Sanderson, Assistant

Commercial Officer, North Eastern Region, BR, took over as General Manager of the Easingwold Railway, and continued in this position until the closure.

At a meeting of shareholders, in the summer of 1952, there was a proposal to close the railway, but it was decided to review the situation in three months time. The result was a decision to keep going, and the Spring of 1954 revealed that goods traffic was being steadily maintained, although the railway had taken on a very 'rural' aspect, somewhat akin to the immortal Bishop's Castle Railway. The track was pretty solid, but uneven, and the telegraph posts no longer supported any wires. Little painting had been done since the War years – indeed, finances had not allowed for this.

Much to most enthusiasts' surprise, visits during the next two years proved the line still to be running, but Mr Bell's place as station master was taken over by Mr L.J. Jackson (BR) who spent five days a week at Easingwold, and then returned to his BR job at York on Saturdays – a rather unique arrangement! The Rail Strike of 1955 had caused some loss of revenue to the Easingwold Company, but a year later, by a strange trick of fate, the petrol shortage arising from the Suez crisis caused a minor, but welcome, boost to the traffic, which in recent years had included sugar beet, potatoes, and carrots, as well as thousands of boxes of live chicks from the nearby poultry farm of Messrs Spink. It was becoming evident, however, that the sands of time were running out, for the total deficit at the end of 1956 had reached the figure of £12,245, with the annual loss amounting to something between £1,500 and £2,000.

By now, the old ex-GCR Compo. had finally been pensioned off, and its place taken by a modern ex-LNER van – easily the smartest piece of equipment on the line! – although the weigh office, now used as the company's HQ was still in fair condition.

In September, came talk of early closure, and on Friday 27th December, 1957, the last train pulled out of Easingwold station never to return. It consisted of 0–6–0 'J72' class locomotive No. 68698, several wagons of sugar beet (Mr W. Pearson Brown was the last person to pay for goods in transit by train), and the four wheel van carrying Directors, the General Manager and various invited guests.

The *Northern Echo* for the following day summed it up most aptly under the headlines 'Easingwold Railway died quietly – but it deserved a better end. Even mourners were shut in guards van'. The special correspondent went on in some style:

> There was an air of quiet melancholy, a quality of anti-climax, about the closing down ceremony for the Easingwold Railway in North Yorkshire yesterday. One felt it deserved a better end. Somehow the ceremony lacked the valiant spirit of a proper Yorkshire funeral where there is a ham and a small port to fortify the bereaved. 'The mourners' made the last three mile trip from Easingwold to Alne in a closed-in guards van. This in itself hardly gave them the best chance to see the last of the line. 'Noises off' were supplied by fog signals on the metals and a few brave blasts on the whistle of the engine.
>
> In the end it was rather sad. There were some people yesterday who could remember the glorious beginning, when the children of Easingwold were marching

to the station, waving flags and in their best clothes, to take a first ride to Alne.

Travelling on the footplate with George Paragreen was Mr Sydney Smith, a retired Post Office official aged 85, of Market Place, Easingwold. He was given this honour because as a lad in his teens he took over the first engine from NER men at Alne and drove it on its inaugural journey to Easingwold.

Another traveller was Mr H.F. Sanderson, Assistant Commercial Officer, British Railways, North Eastern Region who had been manager for the Easingwold Company in recent years. He told the reporter: 'The closing of the line was inevitable, mainly because traffic has fallen to such a low level that it can be handled more economically and efficiently by British Railways through York and other rail heads on the main line'.

Mr Sanderson mentioned that British Railways have offered jobs at York to the Easingwold staff. The veteran of them all, Mr Jack Morse, aged 81, will be retained at Easingwold as British Railways agent. There was nothing remarkable to see . . . just an old engine bearing a notice 'The Easingwold Flyer', a chalked inscription 'Sic-Transit-Gloria', and the enigmatic words 'City of Tears' scrawled on the side. I asked George Paragreen about the last one. 'Easingwold will find out', he said and grinned darkly.

It was rather ironic the BR relief crew did not turn up, so the fire had to be dropped on 68698 and the Easingwold footplate crew had to walk back to the station to get a lift home by car. It was – the end of the line – and of 66 years of loyal service to the public – so sad it left debts of nearly £17,000, £13,000 to British Railways and a mortgage of £3,800.

The end is nigh! A rather forlorn No. 2 with 'Easingwold' erased from its tank and coupling rods removed for towing, stands outside Darlington, North Road 1947/48 awaiting scrapping. *G. Horsman Collection*

Chapter Seven

Personalities

The story of a homely little railway such as the Easingwold line would not be complete without at least a brief reference to the people who guided its fortunes, and carried out its day-to-day operation.

The original Directors have been detailed in Chapter One. The Chairman was J.H. Love, *Bradshaw's Railway Manual* for 1894 indicates that Thomas Hodgson, of Easingwold, had also later become a Director. By 1910, there had been various changes, with only Sir G.O. Wombwell left of the original directorate. F.J.H. Robinson, Esq., had succeeded J.H. Love as Chairman – a position he retained until 1930 – and the remaining Directors were E.B. Hicks, Junr, and James Haynes, both of Easingwold, and J.J. Penty of Darlington.

Later George Henry Coates, Secretary and Manager from 1926 to 1948 joined the Board, and was a Director for many years until his death in 1952. His widow, Margaret, recipient of his £2,000 worth of shares in the company, took his seat on the Board in 1953, and from 1955 to 1956 she was in the unusual position of being the only member of the Board. However, this position was shortly afterwards remedied by the election of two new Directors – Mrs W. Allison and Mr A.R.G. Hawkins – and Mrs Coates became the last Chairman, from 1956 to 1957, in place of R.E. Smith, Esq. (Chairman, 1930 to 1955).

The first Secretary and Manager of the line was John Hetherton, an accountant, of York, who held office from 1891 to 1893. His successor was Dr Edward Buller Hicks, a local practitioner, and Medical Officer for Easingwold. This gentleman, for many years, undertook the secretarial work in an honorary status, but later on received a salary. His term of office as Secretary and Manager, from 1893 to 1925, covered the most prosperous period of the railway's history.

Dr Hicks was succeeded by George Henry Coates, who was appointed in 1926, and remained in charge of affairs until ill-health caused his retirement at the end of 1948. Mr Coates served with the NER and LNER for a period of 50 years, and was Area Senior Accountant when he retired. He had audited the Easingwold Railway's accounts for many years prior to becoming the line's Secretary and Manager. During his 22 years in office, at Easingwold, he did not spare himself in his endeavours to keep the little railway on a sound basis. He passed away in February 1952, at the age of 83. Mrs M. Coates' association with the railway began when, as a girl in her teens, she used to do secretarial work for Dr Hicks, and she has been connected with it, one way or another, since just after leaving school.

There were seven station masters in the company's history, of whom Mr Thornton was the first, to be followed successively by Messrs Raine, J.W. Harnby, T. Shipley and A. Caygill – who held the post for many years. The last officials, Messrs Bell and Jackson, were actually loaned by British Railways.

The drivers in the earlier years included Messrs J. Danby, Shaw, and Clare. Jack Danby drove the engines for a considerable number of years, and

The Railway Year Book, for the years 1909–1915, both inclusive, lists him as 'Locomotive Superintendent' from 1898 to 1908, succeeded by Mr E.L. Witz in the period 1909–1915. Firemen included Messrs 'Billy' Smith, F. Callaghan, J. Brett, Clay and Sydney James Lusher. Bertram Lawson of Raskelf fired for Jack Danby before becoming a driver in the years running up to World War I. He subsequently left to join the Lancashire & Yorkshire Railway.

Probably the best known personalities on the line, however, were Mr George Paragreen and Mr Edward Morse (always known as Jack). George, the son of a platelayer, was born in the gatehouse of Crankley, where, in later years, his sister Mrs Emily Dalton was the crossing keeper, and he had his first ride on the engine when he was a young lad at school. In due course, he joined the Easingwold Railway, and for 10 years fired and 'washed out' 'No. 2' for Jack Danby, later on becoming the sole driver. A cheerful personality, he served over 40 years on the footplate, and despite thousands of journeys over the 2½ mile of single track, he always found his work anything but monotonous.

George was a popular local man, and he and his wife were recalled with very fond memories by Harry Ray who was evacuated with his brother from Hull to the peace and quiet of Easingwold during the last war, and lived with the Paragreens in their railway cottage. He recalled that George was quite a marksman, and on most days his folding shotgun was in the locomotive cab, or concealed under his overalls.

He rarely lost an opportunity to bag a little extra to help out the wartime rationing. George was one of the first people to turn out when the old station building went up in flames, but, sad to relate, he suffered a stroke soon afterwards and died in hospital during September 1967. This brought to an end his family's involvement with the railway's history as his father W. Paragreen had helped to lay the original track in 1891 and, as former plate-layer, continued to maintain the right of way for over half-a-century, assisted during that time by Mr B. Britton.

Edward (Jack) Morse was a Shropshire lad born in Ludlow, and as a youth he joined the GWR at Ludlow in 1892. Later he transferred to Shrewsbury shed before moving on as a passed cleaner/fireman to the London & North Western Railway at Crewe. On three occasions he assisted with the cleaning of Queen Victoria's Royal Train engine of 1897, the famous Webb Compound, *Greater Britain*.

For many years a framed colour print of the engine occupied a prominent place in the Morse's parlour. The picture along with the large elaborate certificate he originally purchased in 1900 to record his admission to the Associated Society of Locomotive Engineers & Firemen, were both presented to the old York Railway Museum.

Young Morse moved to Easingwold in 1902 after his mother took over the license of the Commercial Hotel in the Market Place. He joined the Easing-wold Railway in 1906, initially to take charge of the station coal depot. Over the next 51 years he tackled just about every job called for – driver, guard, ticket collector, and did a lot of clerical work on the parcels side. It was often recalled by the members of staff that his handwriting was a delight to see. His other trademark was his boots, always polished up to a Guardsman's standards.

An early riser all his life, usually around 5.30 am, he made a good sideline of collecting mushrooms and regularly had a couple of boxes on the way to market on the first train of the day. A keen cyclist up to the age of 85, he was proud of using the same bike for over 60 years! This remarkable man was probably the oldest railway employee in England; even after the closure of the railway he took over the post of station agent at Easingwold for the North Eastern Region of British Railways. The job involved the organisation of the collection and delivery of parcels and goods using York-based motor vehicles, as well as handling the grain sack hire on behalf of BR. This job entailed his daily attendance at the station up to 1964 when the service ended and he retired after 56 years' service, aged 87, a year after his Diamond Wedding Anniversary celebrations. He left two sons and a grandson working for British Railways to carry on the family tradition, while he enjoyed working in his garden. Mr Morse died on 21st January, 1967, aged 90.

For most of the railway's existence, the staff totalled 12 men (excluding the Company Secretary and the Manager), made up as follows: two drivers, who had to double up as guards, one fireman, one station master, two clerks, four porters and two platelayers. In the lean post-War period these had to be drastically reduced to just four men: driver George Paragreen, Joe Parling, guard, Charlie Squirrell, porter, Jack Morse doing mainly clerical work, and not forgetting Mrs Emily Dalton who looked after the gates at Crankley Crossing. British Railways provided the last station master, Mr Lawrence Jackson, a relief clerk from Helmsley who worked at Easingwold from Monday to Friday and for BR on Saturdays. He was a good choice for this rather unusual arrangement, being a railway enthusiast and skilled modeller and he coped well with the running of this smallest of railways.

A general view of Easingwold yard seen on 20th September, 1952. To the rear of the loading gauge is the former steam wagon shed; the single van is at the 'new' goods wharf with roadside loading stage. *K.E. Hartley*

Chapter Eight

From Closure to the Present Day

In order to go into Voluntary Liquidation, and realise its assets, the company had either to seek Parliamentary sanction to do this, or else become a Limited Company. Winding-up, under the Companies Act, is cheaper and more convenient than with the first-named method.

After the decision was taken to close the railway, a meeting of Directors and Shareholders was held at the Station Hotel, Easingwold, where the procedures for going into Liquidation were discussed with British Railways officials. The outcome was that the British Transport Commission arranged for the Easingwold Railway to be turned into a Limited Liability Company, and the *Financial Times* on 10th January, 1958 recorded that: 'The Easingwold Railway Co., had been registered as a Limited Company, with a capital of £13,500'. Once the formalities had been completed, the disposal of the track, buildings, and land could be proceeded with. £5,000 was realised from the first-named item, which was dismantled by Messrs T.W. Ward & Co. Ltd of Sheffield.

To fill the gap left by the closure of the line, British Railways, York, installed a goods and parcels road service from Easingwold to be handled by Mr Morse as station agent. The usual BR printed 9½ in. × 5½ in. obituary style notices went up to announce the end of the rail service and the alternative arrangements by road:

CLOSING OF
EASINGWOLD STATION

Easingwold Station will be closed as from 28th December, 1957.

Alternative Facilities

Parcels and other merchandise by passenger train (including Passengers' unaccompanied luggage)

A parcels collection and delivery service will operate in the area.
Parcels, etc. addressed 'To be called for' or not requiring delivery should be addressed to or handed in at Easingwold Station where a British Railways Office will be open from 9.30 am to 12 noon each weekday.

Goods Train Traffic

For traffic requiring collection or delivery, a Railway Road Motor service will operate from York station.

Traffic in less than truck loads not requiring collection or delivery may be addressed to or handed in at Easingwold Station British Railways Office between the hours mentioned above.

Traffic in truck loads not requiring collection or delivery should be consigned to or loaded at Alne Station.

British Railways Grain Sacks may be hired and returned after hiring to Easingwold Station British Railways Office.

The District Commercial Superintendent, British Railways, York, (Telephone York 53022 Extension 571) or any Station Master in the area will be pleased to supply further information or, if desired, arrange for a Railway Commercial Representative to call.

The end of a landmark – Easingwold station building on fire, the evening of 13th June, 1967. *C.R. Evers*

The morning after the fire, the two brick chimneys hold together the charred remains of Easingwold station. By the following Sunday, 18th June, 1967, all timber/brickwork had been completely demolished. *C.R. Evers*

The British Transport Commission agreed to pay the Liquidators of the railway the sum of £20 and £25 per annum respectively, plus rates, for the use of the office and warehouse at Easingwold Station. This arrangement continued up to 1964 when Mr Morse finally retired to get on with his gardening. The station yard, auction market and field (which had been rented by George Paragreen) were acquired by Messrs F. Close & Simpson, Estate Agents, for a sum understood to be £3,000. No development work was carried out possibly due to site drainage problems, and it was eventually purchased by Easingwold Rural District Council. The station yard, minus its track remained substantially unaltered for nine years, just slowly becoming more neglected and overgrown, broken fences and creeping dereliction overtaking the buildings.

The most significant event was the fire on Tuesday evening, the 13th June, 1967 when the old station building went up in flames. The timber structure burned so fiercely that nothing could be done to save it by Station Officer George Salton and his local crew assisted by Mr Morse and Mr Paragreen. The cause of the fire was investigated but no suitable explanation was ever found. Next to go, the following year, was the weighbridge office which became so shaky that demolition was essential, but the weighbridge and its scales mechanism were retained.

The four cottages in Raskelf Road, and the two gatehouses, were disposed of, variously, to Mr Spink, Mr Morse, and members of the Paragreen family, at prices ranging from £150 to £350. In 1960, the Midland Bank set up a small wooden office on the old passenger platform, for the convenience of customers attending the Auction Mart, but this was removed about a year later.

The yard itself was for a number of years used as a winter parking by showmen, and occasionally by touring caravans. During the summer of 1968, squatter vans appeared and became such an eyesore that the Council was forced to evict them and enclose the site with stout fences and barbed wire. The showmen were not included in the ban and were allowed back for the winter of 1969.

The station yard area is now an attractive housing development. The only railway building to survive to recent times was the engine shed. This could be seen from the footpath between Nos. 27 and 29, Drovers Court and remained reasonably intact until 1989, but is now just a concrete base with its walls cut down to seven courses of bricks. The trackbed to Alne is now private land; the two crossing keepers' rustic red brick cottages have become pleasant detached houses, and one can just spot the line of the trackbed, but all traces of the level crossing gates have long vanished.

The Alne station site is now part of the new face of British Rail, following the £120 million electrification of the East Coast route which called for the raising of the overbridge to increase headroom for the overhead wires. There is no sign of the main line station or the bay platform, once the terminus of the Easingwold Railway. The ex-North Eastern Region goods shed is still intact and used as a stonemason's workshop.

The Railway Museum of York, opened by the LNER and the forerunner of the present National Railway Museum, absorbed a few of the smaller relics, tickets and photographs, a jack and tool box used for the permanent way maintenance, the old style Easingwold station master's official braided hat, and a works plate from engine 'No. 2' (H.C. No. 608), the latter being the only item on public display.

So, 23 years after closure occurred, there's not a lot left, though older people still recall fond memories of the old 'coffee pot' and the days when 50 to 60 people could be waiting for the train to York on Saturday mornings. Even without a railway however, Easingwold is a delightful old place, and well worth a visit for its own sake.

EASINGWOLD RAILWAY CO.—TIME TABLE.

	a.m.	a.m.	a.m.	am	p.m.	p.m.	p.m.
Leave Easingwold	7.30	8.36	*10.25	11.2	1.15	3.15	5.0
Arrive Alne	7.38	8.44	10.33	11.10	1.23	3.23	5.8
Arrive York	8.6	9.11	.	11.40	1.51	.	6.18
	a.m.	a.m.	a.m.	am	p.m.	p.m.	p.m.
Leave York	7.48	8.40	10.15		.	3.10	5.12
Leave Alne	8.10	9.2	10.40	11.20	1.38	3.37	5.47
Arrive Easingwold	8.18	9.10	10.48	11.28	1.46	3.45	5.55

*On Saturdays leaves 10.10 and arrives at York at 10.43.

Timetable for 1931.

L. & N. E. R.

EASINGWOLD

From Scarborou

THIRD CLASS CONTRACT TICKET.

25 .... Date of Issue........

Holder's Name ....

Rate 1-7-3

This ticket is not transferable, and is issued subject to the notices, regulations and conditions contained in the current Time Tables and Time Bills of the Company.

The Holder must show this ticket to any Officer of the Company when required: in default he will be charged the ordinary fare for the journey travelled.

Initials of Issuing Clerk ....

G. H. COATES, Secretary.

Appendix One

Extracts from Directors' Reports

GROSS RECEIPTS

		1949	1950	1955	1956
		£	£	£	£
Total receipts from passengers		NIL	NIL	NIL	NIL
Parcels, excess luggage, and other merchandise by passenger train		203	213	387	462
Mails and parcels post		43	26	NIL	NIL
TOTAL PASSENGER TRAIN RECEIPTS	£	246	239	387	462
GOODS TRAIN TRAFFIC					
Merchandise (excluding classes 1–6)		1,441	1,053	804	696
Minerals & merchandise (classes 1–6)		301	318	184	242
Coal, coke, patent fuel		332	298	295	271
Livestock		67	138	31	14
TOTAL GOODS TRAIN RECEIPTS		2,141	1,807	1,314	1,223
Total traffic receipts		2,387	2,046	1,701	1,685
Miscellaneous	DR.	2	39	44	38
TOTAL	£	2,385	2,085	1,745	1,723

Locomotive No. 2 at Easingwold with Mr Morse by buffer (c.1933).
Courtesy Mrs M. Coates

PART 16. *RECEIPTS & EXPENDITURE IN RESPECT OF COLLECTION AND DELIVERY OF PARCELS AND GOODS*

TO EXPENDITURE		1949	1950	1955	1956	*BY GROSS RECEIPTS*		1949	1950	1955	1956
		£	£	£	£			£	£	£	£
Maintenance of horse vehicles		8	3	–	–						
Amounts paid for hired cartage		154	185	125	113	Goods train receipts		165	188	125	113
Balance		3	–	–	–						
TOTAL	£	165	188	125	113	*TOTAL*	£	165	188	125	113

MAINTENANCE AND REPAIRS AND LOCOMOTIVE & TRAFFIC EXPENSES

ABSTRACT "A" *1949–50 1955–56*

MAINTENANCE & RENEWAL OF WAY AND WORKS

			1949	1950	1955	1956
			£	£	£	£
Maintenance of Roads, Bridges & Works			NIL	NIL	NIL	NIL
Maintenance of Permanent Way, (Renewals, Repairs)			NIL	NIL	NIL	NIL
Wages			74	–	45	70
Materials		CR.	705	35	14	11
Maintenance of Telegraphs			5	5	6	18
Maintenance of Station Depots, Offices			13	–	4	–
Maintenance of Engine Shed			NIL	NIL	NIL	NIL
TOTALS	£	CR.	613	40	69	99

ABSTRACT "B" *1949–50 1955–56*

MAINTENANCE AND REPAIRS TO STEAM LOCOMOTIVES AND COACHING STOCK

NOTHING WAS EXPENDED ON THESE ITEMS IN THE YEARS:
1949, 1950, 1955, 1956.
(NO DETAILS AVAILABLE FOR THE YEARS 1951–2–3–4–7)

EASINGWOLD RAILWAY – EXTRACTS FROM DIRECTORS' REPORTS – FINANCIAL ACCOUNTS 1949–57 INCLUSIVE

LOCOMOTIVE RUNNING EXPENSES		1949	1950	1951	1952	1953	1954	1955	1956	1957
Wages connected with Steam Locomotive	£	368	363	365	410	410	430	516	535	533
Fuel		573	450	577	511	567	552	521	555	480
Water		10	14	16	16	16	16	16	12	3
Lubricants		44	16	15	17	21	16	19	17	17
Miscellaneous		–	24	36	27	3	6	6	4	5
Hire of Locomotive	CR.	359	871	865	867	883	873	524	527	529
TOTAL		995	1,738	1,874	1,848	1,900	1,893	1,602	1,650	1,567
TRAFFIC EXPENSES										
SALARIES Station Master & Clerk		264	561	689	643	659	749	787	824	844
& Ticket Collectors, Porters, etc.		507	515	521	538	697	631	535	394	387
WAGES Guards		255	241	252	276	270	288	316	323	330
TOTAL		1,026	1,317	1,462	1,457	1,626	1,668	1,638	1,541	1,561
Hire of Stock		–	–	–	–	–	–	–	–	–
Fuel, Lighting, Water & General Stores		1	3	2	3	3	4	5	3	3
Clothing		–	–	–	–	–	–	–	–	–
Printing, Advertising, Stationery, Stamps, Tickets		37	19	4	3	4	4	3	4	CR13
Expenses, Joint station and Junction		60	60	60	60	60	60	60	60	60
Cleansing, Lubrication & Lighting of Vehicles		–	–	–	–	–	–	–	–	–
Miscellaneous		17	36	33	28	30	25	40	63	71
		115	118	99	94	97	93	108	130	121
TOTAL		1,141	1,435	1,561	1,551	1,723	1,761	1,746	1,671	1,682

Appendix Two

Notes on Tickets

As detailed in the text, the general tickets were of the standard Edmondson card design (30.5 mm × 57 mm) basically in a pale green colour, with different colours for special trains.

The contract tickets in the main in red were large (57 mm × 70 mm) but remaining examples have faded to a lighter shade. Some carried the title across the top in Gothic script EASINGWOLD RAILWAY COMPANY. In the early 1930s the cost was £1 7*s*. 3*d*. or 8*s*. 3*d*. for students.

In 1918, Dorothy M. Fox of Coxwold was issued with a 'Periodical Ticket' of folded paper, one mounted in a smart red card wallet (95 mm × 107 mm) this being entitled in gold – EASINGWOLD RAILWAY – CONTRACT TICKET. This remaining example is unstated as regards class but is dated 10th September, 1917 to 26th July, 1918, and cost 15*s*., and was signed by E.B. Hicks, the Secretary and Manager.

The Easingwold Railway newspaper tear-off parcel tickets (80 mm wide × 60 mm) were thin white paper and priced at 1*d*. each. Later LNER versions were far smaller and varied from 8*d*. up to 4*s*.

The pair of early North Eastern Railway coach bodies used as stores near to Easingwold goods shed for many years are here photographed at the end of their useful life.
Photomatic Ltd

Appendix Three

Notes on the Building Drawings

In all cases, except the 'Pre-1944' toilet, they are made from measurements taken from the actual buildings, so far as possible, but, in some cases, heights have had to be computed, e.g. by counting courses of bricks, and by careful scrutiny and checking of all available photographs.

In the case of *the passenger station building*, it was not possible to fully measure this up, but the main dimensions had, fortunately, been recorded before it was destroyed by fire, in 1967. Other measurements have been estimated, partly from these, and are, I believe, substantially correct.

The overall length of the building was 50 ft, with the 4 ft 6 in. wide brickwork of the end chimney stack projecting a further 3 in. beyond this. The width was 13 ft, and it was constructed of tongued-and-grooved boards, on a brick base. The height to the eaves (lower edge) was 11 ft 3 in. – 20 boards – and to the ridge, approximately 17 ft 9 in.

The roof (17 rows of slates, with red ridge tiles) projected approximately 1 ft at both ends and sides, with a few extra inches for the guttering. The brick chimney stacks, 1 ft 7 in. square, were 3 ft 6 in. above the ridge, and the pots were, roughly, 1 ft high. Note that the end pot was square, and the other one round.

All the windows, front and rear, were 4 ft × 6 ft 9 in., outside the frame, except that in the Manager's office, which was 4 ft 6 in. wide.

Two shallow steps led into the Manager's office, but in front of the double doors, there was a concrete ramp on the platform side, and a flight of steps at the rear.

Three vertical battens, on each side of the building, covered the joints in the matchboarding, and over those on each side of the double doors, fallpipes from the guttering were positioned.

Note the economical use of the lamps – that at the rear served to light both the road entrance to, and, the booking office itself. The latter was also partly lighted by the lamp which, on the other side, formed half the illumination for the platform. A lamp on the toilet served for this edifice and the rest of the platform!

The colour scheme for this building, and also the weigh office, is detailed in Chapter Two.

Note: A newspaper report of the fire gave the size of the Station Building as '40 ft × 20 ft', but is definitely incorrect.

The original *toilet* was of similar construction and colour as the Station Building and Weigh Office. I failed to measure up this little erection, pre-war, but from photos etc., I have prepared what I believe to be reasonably accurate sketches. The side facing the track would appear to have been about 9 ft 6 in. long, and upwards of 7 ft high, with a short side panel 3 ft 9 in. long, at one end. The covered portion was about 6 ft 6 in. × 6 ft 9 in., with the height of the flat roof varying from about 10 ft to 10 ft 6 in. This was arranged with a two-way 'fall', for rain water, and was fitted with a wooden 'chimney' ventilator.

The 1944 replacement, in corrugated asbestos sheeting, has a frontage of 9 ft 6 in., and a depth, from front to rear, of 10 ft 9 in. Height to the eaves is 7 ft 6 in., and of the lower edge to the side entry, 6 ft 3 in. This building is unpainted, and retains the natural asbestos colour.

The old *lamp/store hut* was of buff-painted, horizontal, tongued-and-grooved boarding, with a felted 'single fall' flat roof, and was placed 'end-on to the track. Its 1944 replacement, placed parallel to the rails, was of similar style, but with the matchboarding arranged vertically. I have no dimensions of either of these sheds.

PASSENGER STATION BUILDING —

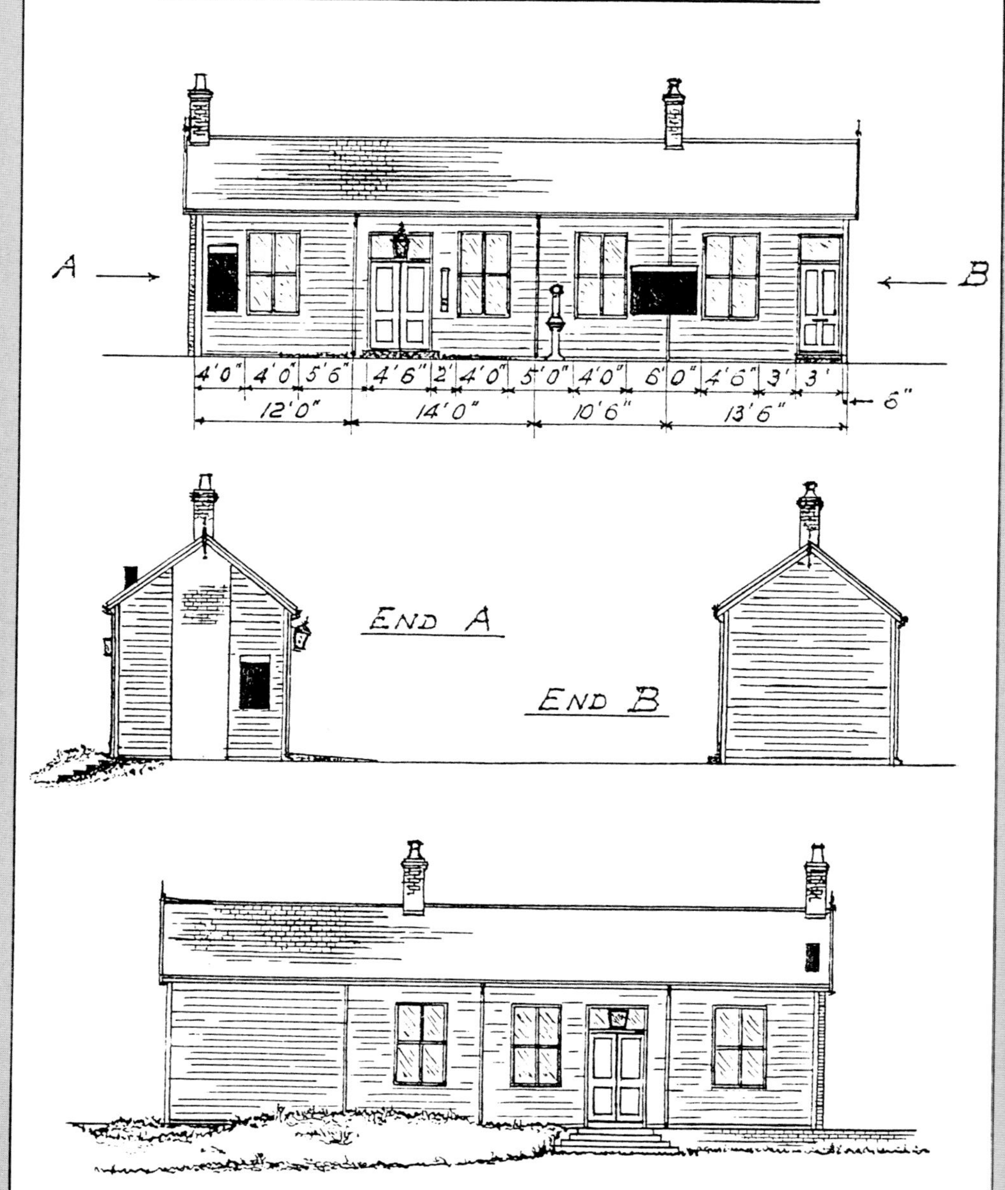

WEIGH OFFICE

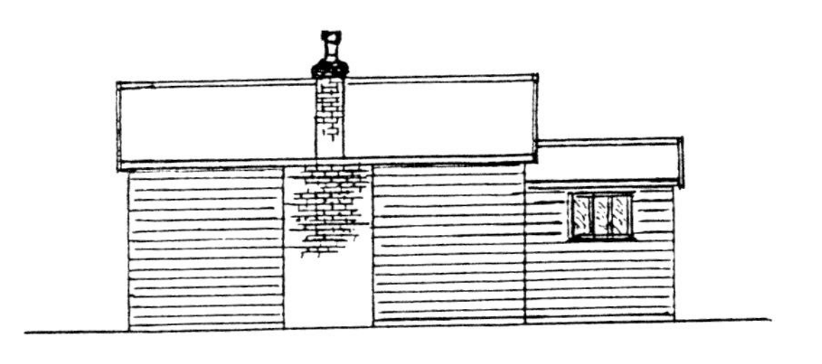

TOILETS

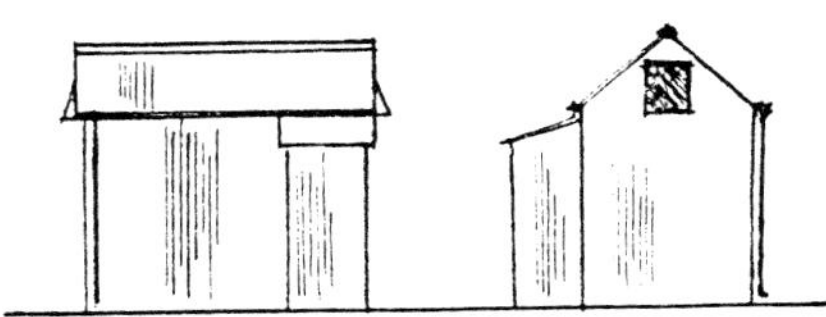

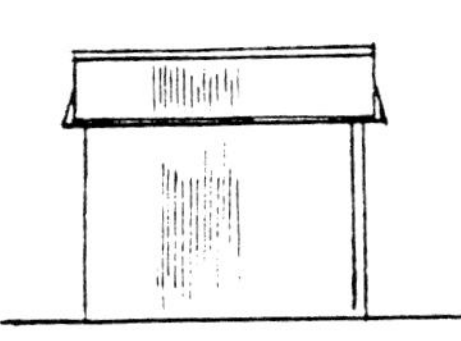

POST 1944

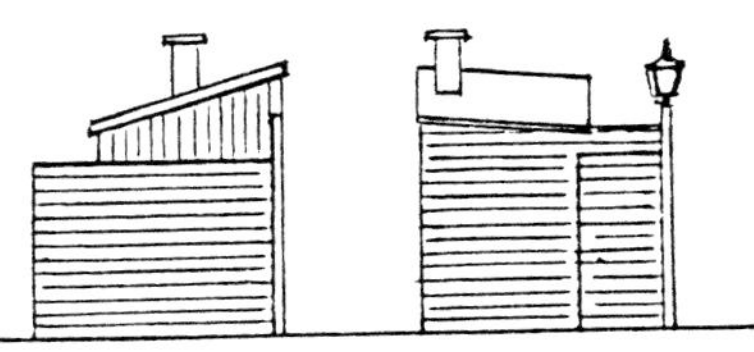

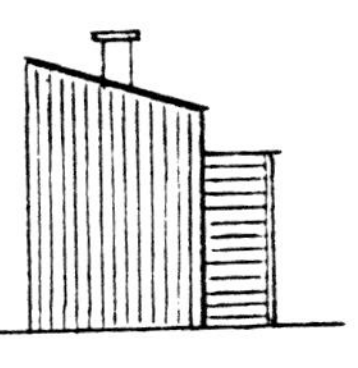

PRE 1944

LNER class 'J71' No. 8297, too tall to enter the engine shed; it had to sleep outside after the day's work. With the shed not in use the flat bottomed rail serving it was left in place when the working lines were relaid in the 1940s. *K.E. Hartley*

The grounded ex-North London Railway composite coach at the back of the Easingwold engine shed, seen in March 1942. The siding to the right is the ramp up to the coal drops. The main line track is looking in good condition with its recently installed second-hand 'Bull Head' rail. *R.C. Riley*

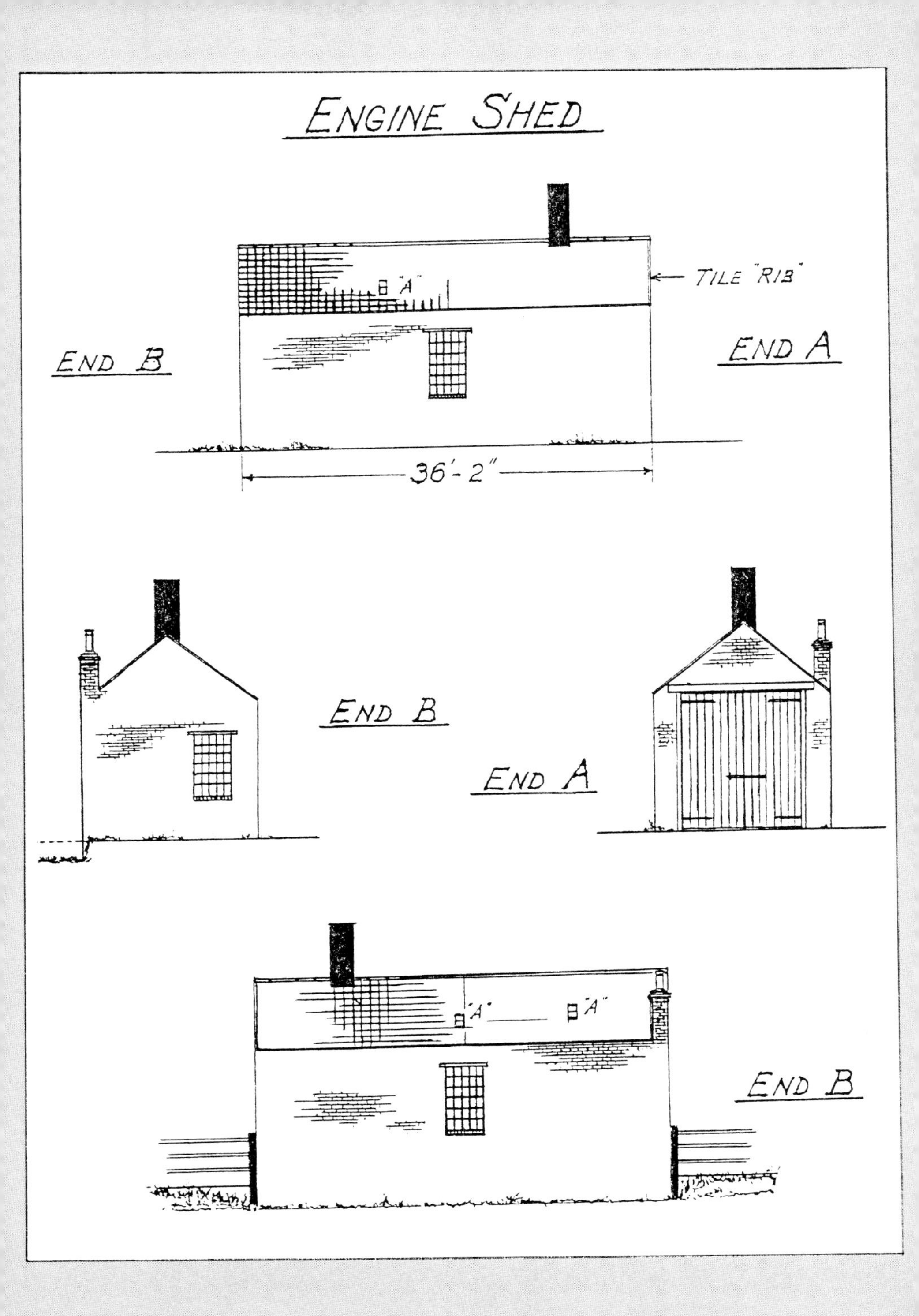
ENGINE SHED
TILE "RIB"
"A"
END B
END A
36'-2"
END B
END A
"A"
"A"
END B

Easingwold Goods shed and loading platform photographed from the buffers on 20th September, 1952. The building was sold in the 1960s to a market gardener, dismantled and re-erected on his adjacent land. *K.E. Hartley*

The steam wagon shed near the gateway to Raskelf Road, Easingwold, in June 1950. It was used during the time the North Eastern Railway operated a road goods service between Easingwold and Brandsby. *K.E. Hartley*

GOODS SHED.

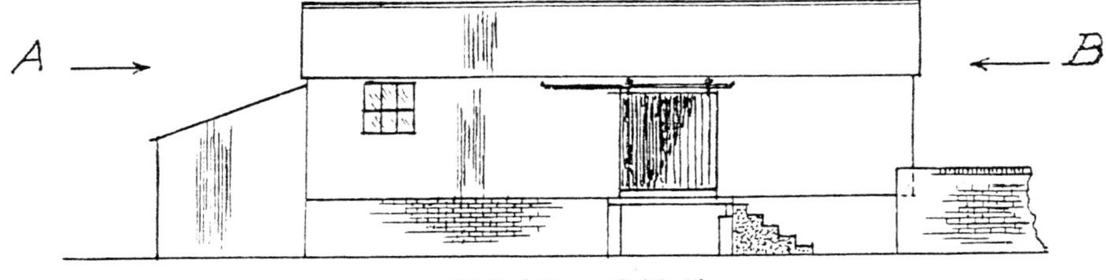

ROAD SIDE

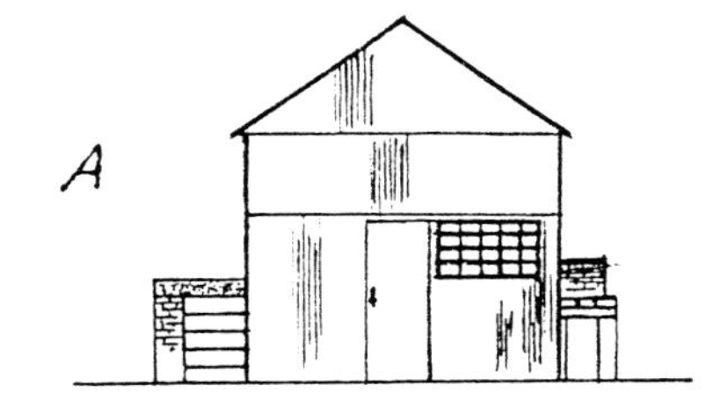

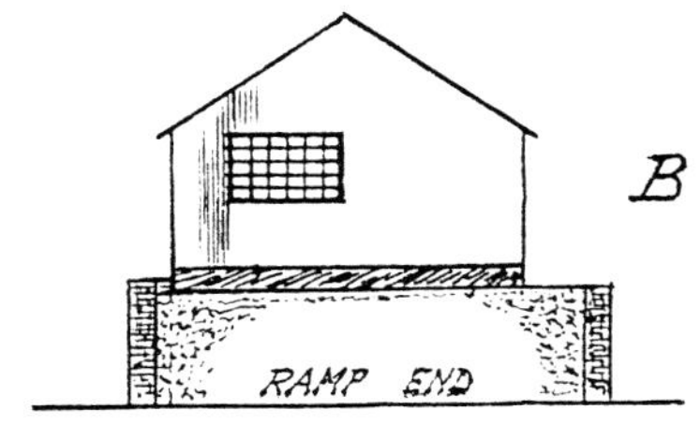

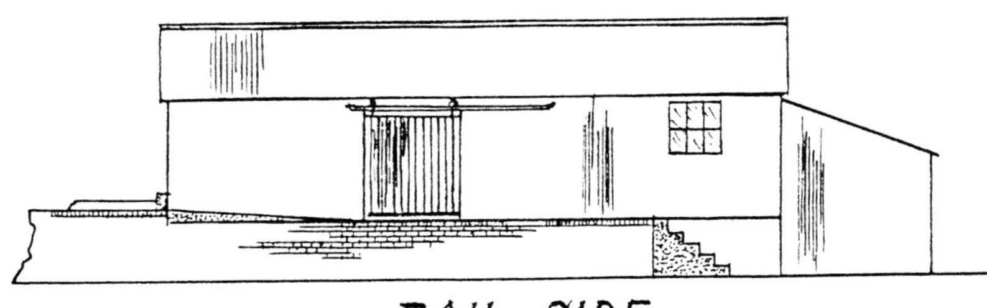

RAIL SIDE

ELEVATION OF END "A" PRIOR TO 1944.

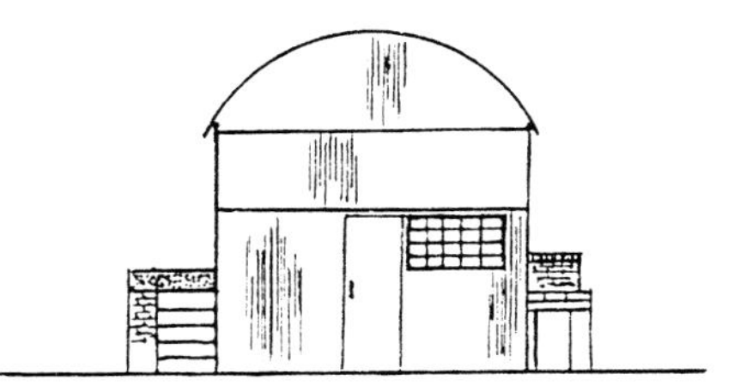

The bread and butter side of railway operation having a quiet day. Easingwold coal drops minus wagons on 1st September, 1951. *K.E. Hartley*

A very early view of *Easingwold* having just arrived at the terminus. To the right is the goods shed and a very well loaded wagon. *Lens of Sutton*

The *platform* on which all the above buildings stood was approximately 300 ft long, by 25 ft wide, and was brick-faced, with a flush top course of bricks on edge, about 1 ft 2 in. wide (1½ bricks).

The main portion of the *weigh office* building measured 21 ft 6 in. in length, and was 12 ft 3 in. wide, with a height of 9 ft to the eaves. The computed height to the ridge was 14 ft. Three large windows, 4 ft 1 in. × 5 ft 9 in., outside the frames, were fitted, with their lower edges roughly 3 ft 3 in. from ground level, and two of these were located centrally in their respective walls. The door – 3 ft over frame – was 1 ft 10 in. from the end of the building, and 2 ft 7 in. from the other end was a smaller window, 1 ft 11 in. × 2 ft 5 in.

At the rear, centrally positioned, was the 4 ft 6 in. wide brickwork of the chimney – the upper part of the stack being 1 ft 7 in. square, and the pot about 1 ft 9 in. high. The brickwork projected slightly beyond the matchboarding, but passed within the wooden edging to the roof, which projected about 1 ft beyond the ends and sides of the building.

A small wash room, 8 ft long × 6 ft 9 in. wide × 7 ft 3 in. high at the eaves, adjoined one end, and had a central window, 2 ft 3 in. × 3 ft 1 in., in the rear wall, 4 ft 9 in. from the ground. There was also a small window, 1 ft 9 in. × 2 ft 3 in. overall, in the end, 3 ft 9 in. from the rear wall, and 5 ft 6 in. from ground level.

Details of the gutter fallpipes are uncertain, apart from that shown on the Front Elevation (R/H end). (This building was completely demolished, during August 1968.)

The main portion of the *goods shed* measured 38 ft × 14 ft 3 in., with the walls 7 ft 10 in. high above the brick base. The estimated height, pre-war, was 15 ft 7 in. from ground level to top of roof and after 1944 this was increased to 16 ft 3 in. The brick base, which on the 'rail' side also formed part of the platform, was 3 ft 9 in. high.

The sliding wooden doors, 6 ft wide, by 7 ft high, were hung from a runner-iron about 13 ft in length.

The side windows, with two intermediate sash-bars, were glazed with over-lapping panes, and measured 3 ft 3 in. long, by 3 ft 6 in. deep. they were 4 ft above the base, and positioned 3 ft 5 in. from the end of the building, on the 'road' side, and 4 ft on the 'rail' side. There was an end window 4 ft 9 in. × 3 ft 1 in. deep, (6 × 5 rows of glass) at the 'platform' end.

The lean-to extension was 9 ft 6 in. long, and 14 ft 3 in. wide, the height at its lower edge being 7 ft 6 in. It had a central, plain, wooden door, 2 ft 8 in. × 7 ft, and a window 4 ft 6 in. long × 2 ft 6 in. deep, abutting the door frame, approximately 4 ft 9 in. above ground level, and 1 ft 3 in. from the edge of the lean-to.

Since the World War II years, both Shed and Lean-to were finished in black, except for the new asbestos sheeting on the roof and end – these were left 'natural'. Window glazing bars were white.

Pre-1944, the round-topped roof was, like the rest of goods shed (including the doors), covered with corrugated iron sheeting. There were then no windows at all in the main part, only in the lean-to, and the colour was maroon all over. The concrete ramp on the 'rail' side of the shed appears to have been a war-time addition.

The platform, or wharf, measured about 135 ft from end 'B' of the shed to the bottom of the ramp, and was 20 ft wide. The brickwork was 4 ft 8 in. high on the 'track' side, and 5 ft 6 in. on the other side, and was edged – like the passenger platform – by 1½ rows of bricks, on edge, i.e. about 1 ft 2 in. wide.

There was a timber post-and-rail fence on the 'road' side, wth 19 posts, spaced at roughly 6 ft 9 in. centres. Five of these posts were about 11 ft high, and the other fourteen were 9 ft 3 in., with four, and three, horizontal rails, respectively. (The longer posts were all at the 'shed' end.)

This wharf was the original one, built for the opening, but increasing traffic appears to have made a second one necessary during 1900, and this is said to have been completed by the end of that year. During the Boer War, large numbers of horses for war service were put on rail from Easingwold, and as many as 300 are stated to have been dealt with in a single day, from the 'new' wharf. During 1943–4 this platform was renovated, and the sides were faced with concrete. It has a length of approximately 175 ft, and there is still a loading stage at the inner end, right by the side of Raskelf Road, adjacent to the side of the Steam Wagon Shed.

Built of common red brick, the *engine shed* had a length of 36 ft 2 in., a width of 15 ft 7 in. and was 12 ft 6 in. from ground level (on the 'rail' side) to the top of the side wall. The other side wall extended about 2 ft lower, to field level, but note that there was no supporting brick wall to the adjoining track bed here.

The forge chimney brickwork was 1 ft 7 in. square, and 16 ft 6 in. high (18 ft 6 in. from field level), with a 2 ft pot of about 1 ft diameter. The three window openings were 3 ft 2 in. × 5 ft 8 in., the side ones having their top edges 2 ft 4 in. below the wall top. There was a 3 in. timber top sill, but none at the bottom – merely a course of sloping-faced bricks, set on edge. The end window was similar, but was set 1 ft lower in the wall.

The red pantile roof was virtually flush with the side and end walls, and had 11 × 50 rows of tiles. The ridge tiles span 2 pantiles. There were three pairs of glass tiles in the roof, as shown at 'A', 'A', 'A' – on the 'field' side, 13 rows of pantiles separated the pairs of glass tiles. The wooden smokestack was roughly 2 ft square, with its centre line approximately 7 ft 6 in. from the end of the shed, and it stood 4 ft 6 in. above the ridge.

Brickwork on each side of the double timber doors was 2 ft wide. The jambs were about 7 in. thick, and there was an 8 in. baulk over the opening, approximately 12 ft above the track. The doors had a total width of 10 ft 4 in., and were braced on the inside by four cross battens and three diagonal ones.

Note that this building was not provided with guttering or fallpipes.

The metal window frames, and all woodwork except the smokestack (black), were red (maroon, when new).

This shed was not the original engine house. It is understood that the first building, on the same site, was a corrugated iron structure, and was somewhat smaller. Apparently, a wagon was being moved off the coal drops, by hand, and somehow 'got away' down the incline, gaining such momentum as to cause it to jump the track and crash into the side of the engine shed, which was, evidently, pretty badly damaged.

It seems likely that the present shed was placed slightly further away from the coal drops turn-out than was the first one, but to make sure that no repetition of the disaster could occur, catch points were installed on the incline, so that any runaway would be deflected away from the 'main line'. It is said that the trees at the side of the incline were left in position in order that any deflected wagon would be stopped by them, and not roll into the adjoining field!

'Railway Cottages' were not built at the opening of the railway, but appear to have been erected in the very early 1900s – probably 1902–5. The 'Station Hotel' dated from about 1892. This was not, of course, a railway property, but the date is of use in connection with establishing the period of old photographs.

Bibliography

The main known articles and references concerning the Easingwold Railway are listed below:

Railway Magazine (illustrated articles): Dec. 1917, Feb. 1930, Apr. 1954.
Locomotive Magazine (illustrated articles): Mar. 1912, Oct. 1929.
British Railways (NER) Magazine (illustrated article): Jan. 1959 'Adieu to the Easingwold Railway'.
Railway World: May, 1954; *The Dalesman*: Feb. 1958; *S.L.S. Journal*: Aug. 1948, Nov. 1948, May 1949; *Modern Transport*: (15th April, 1944).

Articles and other References appear in the files of the *Yorkshire Gazette*, *Yorkshire Post*, *Yorkshire Evening Press*, *Northern Echo*, *Sunday Dispatch*, and the *Easingwold Advertiser*.

Light Railway Handbooks (Oakwood Press).
More Unusual Railways (F. Muller, 1960).
Branch Line Album (Ian Allan, First Series, 1962).
Service Suspended (Ian Allan, 1951).

Locomotive No. 2 with the Railway's name painted out, parked near the locomotive coaling point, with a NER coal wagon on the coal drops to the rear.

J.G. Vincent (R.C. Riley Collection)

C294

INDEX